TO:
Me ♡

FROM:
God, Mom + Dad

DATE:
05/08/2020

new beginnings

DEVOTIONS FOR
NAVIGATING THE TURNS
IN THE ROAD OF LIFE

CAROLYN LARSEN

ILLUSTRATED BY AMYLEE WEEKS

CHRISTIAN ART
PUBLISHERS

Published by Christian Art Publishers
PO Box 1599, Vereeniging, 1930, RSA

© 2018
First edition 2018

Printed in China

ISBN 978-1-4321-2884-5

18 19 20 21 22 23 24 25 26 27 – 10 9 8 7 6 5 4 3 2 1

Table of contents

The Life of Joseph

Genesis 37, 39-47

Moses' Work Begins

Based on Exodus 1:22-2:10

Moses and the Burning Bush

Based on Exodus 3

Red Sea Miracle

Based on Exodus 13-14

FOOD IN THE WILDERNESS

Based on Exodus 16

JERICHO AND RAHAB

Based on Joshua 2, 6

DEBORAH

Based on Judges 4-5

RUTH AND NAOMI

Based on the Book of Ruth

HANNAH'S PAIN

Based on I Samuel I

ELIJAH AND BREAD FOR A WIDOW

Based on I Kings 17:8-16

QUEEN ESTHER

Based on the book of Esther

ELIZABETH AND ZECHARIAH

Based on Luke I

ANNOUNCEMENT OF JESUS

Based on Matthew 1:18-25; Luke 1:26-56

WOMAN AT THE WELL
Based on John 4:1-26

JAIRUS AND HIS DAUGHTER
Based on Mark 5:22-43

WOMAN WITH THE ISSUE OF BLOOD
Based on Mark 5:25-34

WIDOW'S OFFERING
Based on Mark 12:41-44

THE GOOD SAMARITAN
Based on Luke 10:30-37

MARY AND MARTHA

Based on Luke 10:38-42

A WOMAN WASHES JESUS' FEET

Based on Luke 7:36-50

ZACCHAEUS

Based on Luke 19

JESUS FEEDS THE 5000

Based on John 6:1-13

LAZARUS
Based on John 11:1-44

THE STORY OF DORCAS
Based on Acts 9:36-43

SAUL'S CONVERSION
Based on Acts 9

PETER IS AN ANSWER TO PRAYER!
Based on Acts 12

morning

-BY MORNING-

new

mercies

-I SEE-

LAMENTATIONS 3:23

THE STORY
OF THE FIRST SIN

based on Genesis 2-3

THE STORY OF THE FIRST SIN
Genesis 2-3

God created Adam and Eve. He made the Garden of Eden for them to live in. It was beautiful and had everything they needed to live ... beautiful trees that grew fruit for them to eat ... a river of clean water to drink. They had a wonderful life there.

God told Adam and Eve they could eat fruit from any of the trees in the Garden, except one. His one rule was about the tree in the center of the Garden. It was the Tree of the Knowledge of Good and Evil. God told them to stay away from that tree. They could not eat its fruit. If they did, God said they would die.

Life was wonderful until they disobeyed God's one rule. It happened when the serpent challenged what God had said. "God didn't really mean that you can't have that fruit. It will make you as smart as Him. He would want that for you!" the serpent hissed. It didn't take long for the serpent to convince Eve that they wouldn't really be in trouble if they ate the fruit of the forbidden tree. She took a bite and then convinced Adam to have some, too.

Of course God discovered what they had done. Adam said, "The woman You gave me made me do it." Eve said, "The serpent tricked me." God punished their disobedience by making them leave the Garden. He even put an angel guard at the gate so they couldn't come back in. They had to find a new home and work hard to have food. Their relationship with God was broken. Everything was changed.

YOU WIN OR LOSE BY WHAT YOU CHOOSE

When life takes an unexpected turn it can be tempting to blame someone else ... "if my spouse had done THIS ... or if I knew you wanted it THAT way ... or if my boss had told me THIS ... then, of course, things would have turned out different." However, in reality you simply don't want to admit that your own choices got you into the mess you're in. Oh my yes, it's just easier to push the blame onto someone else.

Adam and Eve tried that. Eve blamed the serpent for tempting her and Adam blamed Eve for giving him the fruit. Neither wanted to admit that their own personal choices were the cause of the changes in their lives.

Everything in their lives – from their living situation, livelihood, even clothing was totally and completely changed because of their own personal choices. It did no good to blame anyone else.

Here's the thing – you stand before God alone because you make your own choices and yes ... there is always a choice. It may not be an easy one, but there is a choice. What you choose often determines what comes next.

NO WOMAN IS AN ISLAND

Connections are great, aren't they? Whether it's family, friends or co-workers, it's wonderful to realize you aren't journeying through life alone because people care about you and are there to share your life. Yeah, it's great. Except for the flip side, which is that you're not alone. Oops, did that sound just like the great side? It kind of is — you aren't alone. No man (or woman) is an island. We're in this thing called life together. That means that the choices you make affect not only you but can domino into other people's lives and situations.

That certainly happened with Adam and Eve. Their choices changed their lives and the lives of every person who has lived since them. Otherwise we might all be snuggled together in the Garden of Eden.

So while you may justify your choices by saying no one is affected but you … it just isn't so. People around you are affected because they care about you. If their lives are intertwined with yours then their situations, finances and health may also be affected. When that happens you must take responsibility, confess and apologize and work toward restoration. Of course, the most important confession is to God and restoration will come only through His work in your life.

LOOKING FOR THE GOOD

Can good come from change? Of course it can but the difficult thing is that the good may only come through an attitude adjustment. You must look for the good even as you accept the change.

We don't know what Adam and Eve's attitudes were when they were put out of the Garden. Perhaps there were days when their guilt for disobeying God was overwhelming. Was there any good in their changes? Yes ... they still were part of God's story; in fact the beginning of the human part of God's story. They were able to work, find food and survive. They had a family (which had both good and bad outcomes). It's most likely that they still had a relationship with God, especially if they confessed and repented; after all He loved them.

What do you do when your choices lead to painful changes? Start with admitting your part in the situation, confessing to God and anyone else involved then asking forgiveness (and mean it). Be open to whether there's anything you can learn from the experience and then look for the positives in your new situation. Your positive attitude, humility and open mind might just be the key to finding the good.

i will
-WALK BY-
faith
EVEN WHEN I
cannot see

2 CORINTHIANS 5:7

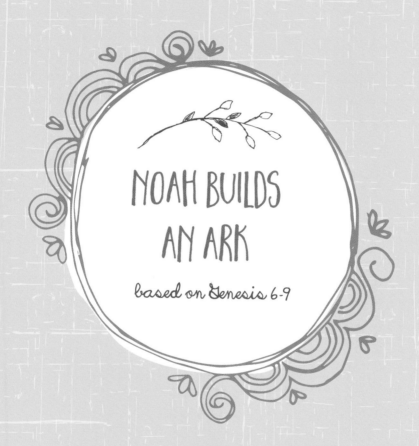

NOAH BUILDS AN ARK

based on Genesis 6-9

NOAH BUILDS AN ARK
Genesis 6-9

God was unhappy with the way people were living. He wanted to tell them to shape up. But no one paid any attention to Him. They didn't care about obeying Him. People had become selfish and self-centered. Finally God decided to wipe out everything He had made and start over.

He went to the only man who still obeyed Him and said, "Noah, a big flood is coming. Everything will be destroyed. But, since you love and obey Me, I want you to be safe. Build an ark, Noah. A big one. I've got a plan."

Noah built the ark just as God told him to. Since none of his friends listened to God, they must have thought Noah was crazy ... until the ark was finished. Then God sent a male and female of every kind of animal to go inside it. Next He told Noah and his family to go inside. When the eight of them were in, God Himself closed the big door of the ark.

Immediately it started to rain. Rain fell for 40 days and 40 nights. When the rain stopped God told Noah to stay inside the ark until the floodwaters were gone. Ten and a half months after they went in the ark, Noah and his family could finally leave it. Everything they had known was gone. Their town. Their home. Their friends. Everything. Starting over was the only option. God promised Noah that He would never send a flood so big that it destroyed the whole world again. He put a rainbow in the sky as a sign of that promise. He said, "When you see a rainbow, remember My promise. Now go on, start new lives and keep loving and obeying Me."

STARTING OVER

No matter what the reason for it, starting over is usually not easy. Sometimes a broken relationship necessitates a start over. Sometimes it's a job change. Sometimes you just want a fresh start. If you've ever started over somewhere you know how hard it can be to make new friends, find a church, find where you fit in, learn where everything is — grocery store, doctor, post office. Everything is brand new and yeah, it is difficult.

Noah and his family surely did face the challenges of starting over. Think about it — everything and everyone they knew was gone. Family members — gone. Friends — gone. Their homes — gone. They knew it was going to happen, too, but they couldn't do anything to stop it.

Wait a minute though. Look at the other side. God saved Noah and his family from the flood. He protected them by providing the opportunity for a new start. They had life. They had each other. Most important they had God.

When you face the challenge of a new start, even if it's due to a painful situation, pay attention to what God may have saved you from. Look for the opportunities in the new start. And, remember ... He is with you each step of the way.

WAITING FOR THE OTHER SHOE TO DROP

The anticipation of what's coming may be worse than the actual event. You know a change is coming but you don't know when or how difficult it's going to be. Your mind constantly wanders to playing out different dark scenarios that could possibly happen. The preoccupation with what "might" happen keeps you from being productive in the meantime. It can also keep you from trusting God.

How can you keep yourself from being preoccupied with worry? Look at Noah. He stayed focused on the work before him. God gave him a job to do to prepare for the coming change so he got busy and did it. No doubt he was curious about what was coming. He may have endured harassment from friends and neighbors about building an ark but he did the job God gave him. Then he was prepared for what came.

When you sense a change coming but God has not yet pointed you in a new direction, keep on doing the job before you and focus your energy on obeying His last instruction. Remember the old saying, "It wasn't raining when Noah began building the ark." Prepare as God leads. Worry gets you nowhere.

KNOW YOUR TRIBE

"Why me, God? Why now, God?" Have you ever secretly asked those questions? You know God loves you. You believe it. You trust Him, but sometimes the changes are painful and the new beginnings seem overwhelming and you feel so alone. Guess what ... it's okay to admit that you're tired of holding on. It doesn't mean you don't trust God. In fact, it shows that you do! You're still holding on.

Perhaps Noah and his family got tired of living in the crowded ark for ten and a half months. It was dark, stinky, confining. Maybe they got seasick. Maybe they got tired of only having the seven other people on board to talk with.

Seven of the ark passengers had to trust that God had spoken to Noah. They did. They knew Noah's heart, his character and that he took obeying God very seriously. There's a good lesson in that. Surround yourself with good people who love God and love you. Know your tribe and let them help you through the changes and new beginnings. God put them in your life for a reason. Pay attention to it.

-HE HAS MADE-
EVERYTHING
beautiful
-IN ITS TIME-

ECCLESIASTES 3:11

ABRAHAM, SARAH AND HAGAR

based on Genesis 15-16, 21

ABRAHAM, SARAH AND HAGAR
Genesis 15-16, 21

"Abraham, I promise that you and Sarah will have a child," God said. "In fact, I promise that you will have more descendants than there are stars in the sky." God blessed Abraham and promised to give him great rewards. Abraham was sad that he had no children to inherit his wealth when he died. He and Sarah dearly wanted children so they were thrilled with God's promise.

But, years passed and Abraham and Sarah grew old but still had no children. Then Sarah took matters into her own hands and gave her servant, Hagar, to Abraham. He had relations with Hagar and she became pregnant. Hagar became arrogant that she was giving Abraham a child when Sarah could not so she began treating Sarah with contempt. That made Sarah angry and she insisted that Abraham send Hagar away. He sadly did so. But, God's angel found her and sent her back to them. Soon she gave birth to a boy, Ishmael.

Several years later God repeated His promise of a child to Abraham. Sarah's response was to laugh at the idea that they could have a child when they were both so old. But, just as God promised, when Sarah was 90 years old, she gave birth to a son. Abraham was 100 years old when Isaac was born.

THE MIRACLE OF NEW BEGINNINGS

Think about it — Sarah was 90 years old when she became pregnant! Scripture says she was long past the age of bearing children so she must have gone through menopause. So the new beginning of her becoming a mother was obviously an act of God. The fulfillment of God's promise to Abraham and Sarah was a miracle!

Now, even beyond the miracle of conception, imagine carrying a baby, giving birth and then caring for the child at 90 years old! Energy levels and strength at 90 are surely not the same as they are at 25 or 30.

God promised a change, a new beginning. It was decades later that He delivered that new beginning. He knew how old Abraham and Sarah were going to be. He knew what He was doing. He obviously delivered the strength and energy they needed to endure the experience of parenthood; not only that, He gave them the blessing of enjoying that new beginning. God doesn't do things halfway. If He orchestrates a change He guides you through it.

TAKING MATTERS INTO YOUR OWN HANDS

Maybe your life isn't turning out exactly the way you always dreamed. You had goals. You had dreams. You. You. You. There's the important word – You. Your plan for your life was yours, not God's. So when the temptation hit to take matters into your own hands and force things to turn out the way you want, well look at what happened to Sarah when she did that.

Sarah wanted Abraham to have a child and she felt she would never be able to give him one; even though God had PROMISED them that they would have a family that numbered in the bazillions. So, to get the change in their status that she wanted, she took matters into her own hands and had him sleep with Hagar. Of course, Hagar got pregnant so yes, Abraham had a son. But Ishmael was not the son through whom God's promise would come.

Waiting for God's timing can take patience and trust and confidence. But, it's worth it. Taking matters into your own hands to achieve what you think God should be doing . . . well, bypassing God in the plan of your life will just cause problems. Wait for Him.

LAUGHING AT GOD'S POSSIBILITIES

Who would dare laugh at God? Not you, right? Yeah … even if God whispered to you that your life is going to have the most amazing, life-changing turn around; one that you've dreamed of for years? You wouldn't laugh, even if you've waited years and years and years with no hint of God's promise coming true. OK maybe you wouldn't laugh but would you sniff, snort, roll your eyes, sigh?

Some change seems to happen with no warning or planning. It seems to be spontaneous change. But in the case of Abraham and Sarah having a child, they had years and years to think about God's promise. When they were old – too old to start a family – He restated that promise and … Sarah laughed.

Of course, Sarah's story didn't end with that laughter. God did keep His promise and Abraham and Sarah's life change was realized with the birth of Isaac. Then her laughter came from pure joy and the amazement of a promise kept. The Change-Maker (God) orchestrates changes in His time. So, laugh if you must but keep looking for His timing!

RESIDUAL FALLOUT

As far as we know, it wasn't Hagar's idea to sleep with the boss and become pregnant with his child. She probably didn't have a choice. And yet, the change effected in her life was major.

That happens sometimes, doesn't it? It feels unfair. It feels wrong. Your life change is the residual fallout of someone else's choices. What's your reaction to changes that are brought on by someone else? Anger, resentment or revenge?

Hagar's response was arrogance. After she became pregnant, she got snarky with Sarah and that led to her being sent away. It must have been scary to be a servant, pregnant and alone.

There's an interesting tidbit in this part of Hagar's story. When God's angel came to her, he asked, "Where have you come from and where are you going?" Those questions are important parts of accepting change in life. Know where you came from ... and what your situation was there. Think about where you're going ... and why. Perhaps that question helped Hagar realize her responsibility in being sent away and that she needed to change her behavior to accept the newness of her situation. The angel told her to go back to Sarah and submit to her. Probably a tough thing to do but important for the birth and well-being of her child ... and that was her new beginning.

-UNDER HIS-
wings
YOU WILL
find refuge
PSALM 91:4

TEST OF
FAITH

based on Genesis 22:1-19

TEST OF FAITH
Genesis 22:1-19

God tested Abraham's faith in a very big way. He asked Abraham to sacrifice … kill … his son, Isaac. The son he had waited decades and decades to have. The son he loved deeply. God said, "Take Isaac and go to the place I tell you and sacrifice him to Me as a burnt offering."

Abraham didn't question God. The next day he and Isaac left for the mountain God sent him to. When they got close to it, Abraham told his servants to wait while he and Isaac went up the mountain. "Father, I know we have the fire and the wood for our offering to God, but where is the lamb to sacrifice?" Isaac asked.

"God will provide," Abraham answered.

When they reached the place God told him Abraham prepared the wood for a fire. Then tied his son to the altar and lifted his knife to kill Isaac. "Abraham!" God's angel called, "Stop. Don't hurt the child. Now I know that you truly fear God. You have held nothing back from Him, not even your son whom you love so deeply."

Then Abraham saw a ram caught in the bushes. He caught it and they sacrificed it to God. The place where this all happened is called Yahweh-Yireh which means, "God will provide."

NEW BEGINNING FOR TRUST

This part of Abraham's story is hard. Did God really ask Abraham to kill his own child — the son he had waited decades for? Did God give and then seemingly plan to take away? The honest, hard answer is ... yes. Maybe you're wondering how this was a new beginning for Abraham. It was a new beginning of revelation. Abraham trusted God. He had moved far away from everything familiar at God's command. He had experienced God's promise fulfilled when Isaac was born. So yes, he knew he trusted God. But imagine the sadness and grief that flooded his heart when God asked for Isaac to be sacrificed. Imagine him looking into his son's eyes as he lifted the knife to kill him. It must have taken every ounce of strength Abraham had. But he did it. His new beginning here was that he reaffirmed, for himself, for God and for Isaac that no one and nothing was more important to him than God.

On that day Abraham KNEW that God was first and foremost in his life. It was a new beginning with the affirmation of where his heart was focused. It was also a testimony to Isaac of the importance of trusting God. Thankfully, God provided an animal to sacrifice so the lessons Isaac learned that day were at least two-fold. God first and foremost. Trust Him no matter what and He will provide.

LETTING GO OF SOMETHING WONDERFUL

Are you holding on to someone or something? Is there something about which you say, or don't say, or think ... "God, I'm all Yours. Have Your way ... except please don't touch ... ???" Would you say that person or thing or situation has become more important to you than God? If you can't submit to allow Him freedom to touch it, then maybe you don't feel you can trust Him. Perhaps you fear that He will ask you to let go of it. The love and trust you have for Him is limited and in some way you believe His love for you is limited, also.

Do you wonder how Abraham did it? Could he have gone through with it if God hadn't stopped him? Would you be able to? Hopefully God will never ask you to do something as difficult as sacrificing a child. But, really, every moment of every day, God wants to know that you are completely His. He wants you to trust Him so completely that you hold nothing back.

Do you need to make some changes? Do you need to let go of something and let it be completely God's? Maybe you haven't had any big changes in your life recently but ... maybe you need to make one. Let go. Trust God. Believe in His love for you and those you love. That's a change for the good.

NEW BEGINNING FOR ISAAC

They're watching. The eyes all around you. The people who hear you say that God is Number One in your life. The people who hear you say the Bible is truth. Those to whom you proclaim that God is love. They're watching. Whether it's your children, your parents, siblings, friends or co-workers. They will notice whether your life matches your words.

Isaac was watching Abraham, too. More than likely he had heard Abraham pray, heard him talk about God and seen him study the Torah. He knew God was important to his father. But that day when Isaac saw that his dad, who he knew loved him very much, was willing to sacrifice his life to be obedient to God, things probably became crystal clear to the young boy – nothing is more important than God. Nothing. It's quite possible that it was a lesson Isaac never forgot. So on that day, at that moment, there was a new beginning in Isaac's heart. A new beginning to always put God first ... no matter what.

Remember those who are watching you. May they see truth in your life that brings a new beginning in theirs.

-GOD HAS MORE-

in store for you

-THAN YOU CAN EVEN-

imagine

EPHESIANS 3:20

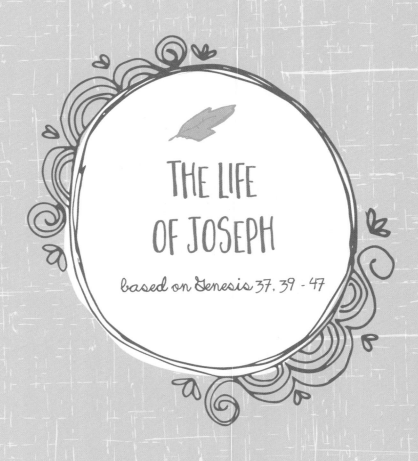

THE LIFE
OF JOSEPH

based on Genesis 37, 39 - 47

The Life of Joseph
Genesis 37, 39-47

Joseph was one of Jacob's twelve sons and of those 12 sons, Joseph was Jacob's favorite. He gave Joseph presents and very openly favored him. That didn't set well with the other boys. He didn't help his own case when he told his brothers about a couple dreams he had where they bowed down to him. His brothers hated Joseph so much that they sold him into slavery then told Jacob that a wild animal had killed him. Joseph ended up in Egypt, a slave in the house of Potiphar. He worked hard and soon his owner put him in charge of all the house workers. But then Mrs. Potiphar unfairly accused Joseph of trying to seduce her and he was thrown into jail.

Joseph continued to live for God even in prison. God honored his obedience by helping him explain some dreams that the Pharaoh had. Pharaoh was so impressed that he pulled Joseph out of prison and made him second in command of the entire country! Joseph had a plan to save the people of Egypt from starving to death in a drought that was coming.

His brothers came to Egypt to buy food so they wouldn't starve. It was Joseph they had to do business with though they didn't recognize him. But Joseph recognized them! He could have had them thrown in jail. He could have sent them home to starve. But he didn't. He forgave them and said, "What you meant for evil, God meant for good." He brought his father, his brothers and all their families to Egypt and took care of them.

DOMINO EFFECT

In thinking of Joseph's story you might say that bad things happen to good people. So many bad things happened at the beginning of this part of his story. Start with Joseph's life — he was ripped away from his family, the life of comfort he knew, his freedom and he was sold into slavery. He hadn't done anything wrong, except maybe brag a little bit. But his brothers were fed up with the favoritism their dad showed. So, they made a choice and that meant they had to live with the lie they told Jacob and to live with the uncertainty of whether they caused their brother's death. Jacob had to live with the grief of losing a child … his favorite son. Wow. So much pain.

Do you think your decisions affect only you? Think about a row of dominoes set up on their short sides. Each tall domino represents a person in your circle of family and friends. Independent individuals. However, when that first domino is pushed over, it falls against the one next to it which then tumbles into the next one and on and on. Your choices and decisions do touch the lives of others — those who love you, those you work with, those who watch your life to learn from it. Your choices and decisions can affect a multitude of changes which you do not even imagine.

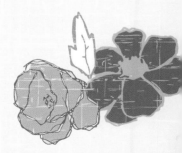

BUT JOSEPH CHOSE THE RIGHT THING

Joseph tried to obey God and live in a way that honored Him. Of course, he was human and, just like any other person, sometimes he made mistakes. But one thing he did right was to refuse the advances of Potiphar's wife. Succumbing to her would have surely landed him in prison or worse ... wait ... he DID land in prison. He did the right thing but was punished because she lied. Where was God in this? Why didn't He honor Joseph's good morals by protecting him?

Yeah ... the hard thing is that bad things do happen to good people. A seemingly bad change came into good Joseph's life (again) because of someone else's action.

Maybe that's happened to you. What do you do with it? It's not fair. It's hard to handle especially if the one who caused your bad change goes along as if nothing ever happened. Look at Joseph's situation — it stunk for sure — for a while. But God was looking at a bigger picture. He saw that the pain of the moment was leading to bigger and better things. Are you in the middle of something pretty tough? Trust the Waymaker for what He has planned for you down the road.

IT'S ALL IN THE ATTITUDE

Attitude. The attitude you take into a changing situation makes a big difference in what happens next. Why? Well, your attitude shows where your heart is in the whole "trusting God" area. For example, look at Joseph. He endured his own brothers selling him into slavery. Then he was unfairly accused of trying to rape his boss's wife and he was thrown in jail. His attitude could have been really bad. Instead, Joseph accepted his imprisonment and worked hard to be the best prisoner they had ever seen. God honored his efforts by helping him interpret a couple of dreams and that served to get him noticed by the Pharaoh. God helped him interpret the Pharaoh's dreams and boom … he's second in command of the country. What would have happened if he had gotten angry, yelled at God, been a lousy prisoner? It could have taken a lot longer for the good to come.

When your life goes from great to not so great, what's your attitude? Do you trust God to bring good from the difficult? Do you accept that He is walking beside you through the difficult times? Is your attitude that of trust, obedience and anticipation?

NEW BEGINNING = NEW CHALLENGES

What an amazing turn of events for Joseph. He went from slave to prisoner to ruler. That last change was awesome! That's a new beginning for sure. It could have been scary, right? What training did Joseph have to be second in command of a big, important nation? Did he have the respect of any of the men he was suddenly ruling over? Seriously, did he know what he was doing? Maybe he was nervous. Maybe he was aware that others didn't support the Pharaoh's decision. Maybe he didn't really know what to do. But, what did Joseph know? He knew that God had opened this door. He believed that God would see him through it. He trusted God.

Joseph's experience is a good reminder that God will not lead you to a new beginning without equipping you to face the challenges. He will not lead you to something new then walk away from you. He walks with you moment by moment. He is the author of new beginnings. He is the equipper for the work.

NEW BEGINNING FOR ... REVENGE?

How do you use the opportunities presented in a new beginning? Joseph became the one in Egypt who was in charge of saving grain to keep people fed during a seven-year drought. When people from other countries came to buy food it was Joseph they had to talk with. So when his brothers came he could have immediately thrown them in prison for what they had done to him. He could have had his revenge. Really, would you have blamed him?

But Joseph didn't do that. Instead, he took the opportunity to provide a new beginning for his father and brothers. By doing that he gave himself a new beginning to – he forgave his brothers for what they had done so any burden of anger was lifted from his own heart.

Joseph's example is a good lesson to take advantage of opportunities to bless other people and provide new beginnings for them, even if they have hurt you. Forgive and move on. It's better for you and for them.

for I know -WHO- holds TOMORROW

MOSES' WORK BEGINS

Based on Exodus 1:22 - 2:10

MOSES' WORK BEGINS
Exodus 1:22-2:10

The Hebrews were in slavery to the Egyptians who were tough taskmasters. But the Pharaoh started growing nervous because the Hebrew women had many babies. He was afraid that as the male babies grew up they would become soldiers and rebel against him. So, he ordered that all the male Hebrew babies be thrown in the Nile River at birth.

One woman, Jochebed, had a baby boy and she knew there was something special about him. So, for three months she hid him from the Egyptian soldiers. Then she put him in a waterproof basket and set him afloat in the Nile River. The baby's sister, Miriam kept watch and saw the servant of an Egyptian princess pull him out of the water. "Shall I get a Hebrew woman to nurse this baby for you?" she asked. The princess thought that was a good idea so Miriam got the baby's own mother to care for him! When he was older he went to live in the palace with the princess. She named him Moses, which means "pulled out of the water." So Moses, the Hebrew boy grew up as an Egyptian prince but he knew of his Hebrew heritage.

THE VERY BEGINNING

Obviously God had a plan for Moses' life from the very beginning. Otherwise he would have been one of the male Hebrew babies who died right at birth. It's interesting to see the thread of God orchestrating His plan, even when Moses was an infant. He saved Moses' life and He made sure Moses had the opportunity to know the history of the Hebrew people.

What does this tell you? Don't discount God's call on your life, even when you are young. Perhaps you can already look back on your own life and see the thread of God's call and direction through the years. That can be encouraging, especially when the going gets rough or when it seems that He has been silent for a while. You can continue being obedient to the last clear guidance you received from Him and be confident that He will continue the good work that He began in you at the beginning.

LOOKING AHEAD

Moses wasn't supposed to live into adulthood. At least if the Egyptian Pharaoh had his way, Moses would have been one of the multitude of Hebrew infants who were drowned in the Nile River. It's interesting that Moses' mother knew he was special. She hid her baby boy, somehow kept him quiet or pretended he was a girl. She quite possibly risked her own life to protect this boy she knew was special. God gave Jochebed the insight to see that He had plans for her boy. She didn't know what those plans were but she felt that big things were ahead for him.

There may be times when God prompts someone to challenge you to consider a change in location, career, ministry or relationship. Or, perhaps you feel the nudge from Him to do that for someone else. It's worth paying attention to because perhaps that person (or you) is God's tool in bringing about a new beginning, much as Moses' mother did in his life. God uses others to speak truth into our lives. Pay attention.

SIDEKICK'S JOB

Moses' sister played an important role in his life and, therefore, in the work God had for him. Her work began early on in her brother's life when he was put in the basket cradle in the Nile River and she kept watch over him. When the Egyptian princess found him, it was Miriam who volunteered to find a Hebrew nurse for him and then got her mother to take care of him. That meant that as Moses grew up he learned about the history of his own people.

So Miriam wasn't the key figure in Moses' ministry but she did play an important sidekick role. That role continued into their adult lives as Moses led the Hebrews out of Egypt.

God puts people together to help and encourage one another, to hold one another accountable and to challenge one another in His work to be done. From the moment Miriam went to the river to watch Moses' basket cradle, she had a "new beginning" in her own life. She walked alongside her brother in the important work God gave him, offering advice and encouragement. It's important to work in community with the people God puts in your life.

-THE LORD IS-

on my side

-I WILL NOT-

fear

PSALM 118:6

MOSES AND THE BURNING BUSH

Based on Exodus 3

MOSES AND THE BURNING BUSH
Exodus 3

Moses left Egypt and became a shepherd. One day Moses was out in the field watching his father-in-law's sheep when he noticed a bush that was on fire but even though it was burning, it never burned up. Moses thought that was odd so he went closer to look at it.

God saw Moses coming close to the bush so He called to him from the burning bush, "Moses! Take your shoes off. The ground you are standing on is holy ground. Listen to Me, I am the God of your ancestors, Abraham, Isaac and Jacob."

Moses was filled with awe that God was speaking to him. He covered his face and didn't dare look at God.

"I've seen the problems of My people, the Hebrews, who are slaves in Egypt. I've heard their prayers for relief and I will help them," God said. "I'm sending you to lead them out of Egypt and into their own land which will be a wonderful place filled with everything they need."

"Me?" Moses asked. "Are You sure You want me to lead them? Who would listen to me? Why would the Egyptian Pharaoh listen to me? Why would the Hebrew people listen to me?"

"Tell the people that 'I AM' sent you. They will listen. I know the Pharaoh won't listen to you but I will be with you. I will make him listen," God said.

So Moses agreed to do God's work.

IS THIS GOING TO WORK?

Moses grew up in the Egyptian palace as the son of the princess and consequently lived a life of privilege. He ran away when things got messy and he feared for his life. Then he had to support himself so he became a shepherd. A shepherd has to be alert and courageous to protect his sheep. Even so, it's a pretty lonely profession.

Then one day God suddenly speaks to him from a burning bush and gives him a job to do that's bigger than anything Moses ever thought of. Moses was scared and he tried to talk God out of giving him the job. But, God's mind was made up.

God had a new beginning for Moses — newer than anything Moses had done before. He was to be the leader of the Hebrew people. He would lead them out of their bondage to the Egyptians. It was going to be a challenge. In fact, it was going to be downright hard. Plus Moses was lacking self-confidence. So what would make God's plan work? Simple — God would. He would be with Moses every step of the way.

God doesn't ask you to do something and then walk away. He will be with you. He will guide, strengthen, intervene … whatever you need. You can trust Him to stick with you and see the work through.

THE BIGGER PICTURE

God's change in Moses' life set up big changes for the entire nation of Israel and that's why God called Moses to do that work. God wanted His people free.

When Moses said, "OK, God, I'll do it," that signaled a major change and new beginning for thousands of people — freedom from slave masters and freedom to live in their own land. Was it easy? Nope. Did they persevere? Only by God's intervention through Moses. Did it take a long time? Yes, because of the people's lack of faith.

When God called Moses to lead Israel out of Egypt, He knew it was going to be a long, involved, dangerous task. That didn't surprise Him. There is the possibility that He may ask you to do long, involved and dangerous tasks, too. They may bring frightening changes in your life situation. Will you be lacking in faith if you are nervous or afraid? No, it's okay to be afraid of a challenge God gives, as long as you don't quit; as long as you keep going to Him (as Moses did) asking for renewed guidance and direction. He won't let you down. Keep seeking Him. Keep moving forward. Keep obeying the direction you have.

MIGHTIER THAN THE

waves of

the sea

-IS HIS LOVE-

for you

RED SEA
MIRACLE

Based on Exodus 13-14

RED SEA MIRACLE
Exodus 13-14

The Israelites were slaves in Egypt for many years. The Israelites begged God to help them and He heard their prayers and sent Moses to lead them out of Egypt. It wasn't easy though. God had to send ten plagues on the Egyptians before the Pharaoh finally let them go. God protected the Israelites from all ten of the horrible plagues. Finally, Moses led the thousands of Israelites out of Egypt and into freedom. They knew that God was with them because a giant pillar filled with His presence led them. It was a pillar of cloud in the daytime and of fire at night.

But the Israelites hadn't been gone long when Pharaoh decided he had made a terrible mistake by letting them go. With them gone, who would do all the work the Israelites had done for him? He and his army went to bring them back.

God led the Israelites to the shore of the Red Sea. They could see the Egyptians coming after them and they were scared. But, Moses said, "Don't be scared. Just watch and see what God will do for you!" God told him to climb up on a rock by the sea and hold out his hand. When he did a strong wind came and blew the waters of the sea into two walls with dry land in between them. Thousands of Israelites crossed through the sea on dry land! But when the Egyptian army followed them the water crashed down onto the army. Every single Israelite got safely to the other side of the Red Sea but every Egyptian soldier drowned in the Red Sea!

PROTECTION/SCARY TIMES/PROTECTION

God sent ten plagues on the Egyptians with the purpose of convincing Pharaoh to let the Israelites go. Each one was more horrible than the one before. It was obvious that God was creating a new beginning for His people because He protected them from each plague. Only the Egyptians experienced them.

When Pharaoh finally let the Israelites leave, God directed them toward the Red Sea. Then they discovered the Egyptians were chasing them. Did God KNOW Pharaoh would change his mind and come after them? Of course He did. So, while the people wondered if Moses had led them to their death, God knew that they were going to see His protection once again.

No doubt it was scary for the Israelites. They may have thought "God wants us free. He's giving us our own land … easy peasy." So when the Egyptian army was rushing toward them and the Red Sea was behind them, did they wonder if God's "new beginning" was not going to happen after all? Yes, they did. But, Moses said, "Just wait and see what God will do." Did he KNOW how God was going to save them? Maybe not at that point but he believed that God WOULD save them.

When you believe God has directed you to a new beginning but life gets messy on the way … hang on. Keep believing. Trust Him. Maybe He is growing your faith as you make the journey.

REMEMBER THE PROMISE

There's a very important statement in this story of the Red Sea protection and it goes back to the start of the story at the burning bush. When God called Moses to lead the Israelites to freedom He promised, "I WILL BE WITH YOU." (Exodus 3:12)

This promise meant that Moses was not going into this challenging new beginning alone. God promised to be with him. That promise was reinforced many, many times during the exodus from Egypt and on into the wilderness wanderings. From miraculous protections to God's presence in a pillar of cloud and fire, Moses and the Israelites saw evidence of God with them over and over. Even when they whined and complained, He was there. Even when they doubted and questioned, He was there. When God says He will be there ... He is.

Do you sometimes wonder where God is as you journey toward new beginnings? Do you question in the seemingly endless trek of job searching; through the struggles of broken relationships; in the agony of health issues ... and on and on. Remember that God IS there. He promised to never leave you or forsake you. He's going nowhere!

BE
joyful
-IN HOPE-

patient
-IN AFFLICTION-

faithful
-IN PRAYER-

ROMANS 12:12

FOOD IN THE WILDERNESS

Based on Exodus 16

FOOD IN THE WILDERNESS
Exodus 16

It had been one month since the Israelites walked out of Egypt as free men and women. One month. God did amazing miracles to secure their freedom. He did an incredible miracle to save them at the Red Sea. He provided water for them from an actual rock. His presence was with them in a pillar of cloud and fire. But when they ran out of food they complained and accused Moses of leading them into the wilderness to die! (Moses was simply following instructions from God.) They even longed to go back to Egypt — to slavery.

God heard their complaints and told Moses that He would send food. There would be meat at night and bread every morning. That's just what happened. God sent quail at night and heavy dew each morning that left white flakes (manna) on the ground when it dried. Moses told the people what God's instructions were. They were to capture the quail at night for meat. In the morning they were to pick up the manna and use it for food. They only needed two quarts for each person and they were not to keep leftovers. On the sixth day they were to pick up enough for two days because on the Sabbath God wouldn't send any. Some people obeyed. Some didn't and the food that they tried to keep spoiled and maggots crawled in it. They disobeyed because they didn't trust God's instructions.

God sent manna for the people for the whole 40 years they wandered in the wilderness.

TRUSTING THROUGH CHANGING TIMES

The Israelites. They had seen God do amazing miracles to set them on a new path and give them their freedom. God gave them chance after chance to trust Him and to see their faith grow stronger. But, God's people failed every single time. When they were trapped by the Egyptians at the Red Sea, when they wanted water, when they were hungry – each time they complained and blamed Moses. Why? They were scared because the changes in their lives and the new beginning they were experiencing did not go smoothly. But then, the God of miracles provided for them by sending food in a totally miraculous way!

Faith is put to the test when the going gets rough. You may believe with all your heart that God has directed a change in your life and you believe that He is present in that change, but what's your reaction when the going gets bumpy … when you're scared or tired or feel alone? Do you look beyond your fear and see His provision and care? Have you seen God provide in a miraculous way to protect you or send you what you need? Look around, you may just see God's presence in a way you never expected … because He loves you and He is with you.

JUST OBEY

God's miraculous provision of providing manna for the Israelites did not come without rules the people needed to obey. They were not difficult rules, really they were just instructions. However, obeying the rules would mean the people trusted Moses ... and God. He said, "Only pick up enough manna to feed your family today. Don't try to store any up for another day." Simple ... except they didn't obey. They were willing to accept God's plan for Moses to lead them to a new beginning. But they didn't trust Him enough to believe He would be true to the details of His word so, they didn't obey the rules.

There will be changes in your life. That's a given. And when the going gets tough or scary or long, what's your responsibility? You can cry, "I don't know what to do!" but that's not true – you do know. You have God's Word that's filled with instructions to trust Him, believe Him and serve Him. And, whatever His last specific instruction to you was you should keep doing it until He tells you to do something else. Don't forget in the hard times that God has a plan and His plan is based on love and helping you become the best you that you can be.

LISTEN

Just listen. That's not so hard, is it? Moses clearly explained God's instructions for receiving the manna God provided each day. All the people had to do was listen ... really listen and then obey what Moses said. Maybe they did listen a little but then thought that little bit of listening was enough and they knew what to do. Or perhaps they listened and ignored. Maybe some didn't listen at all. The thing is their new beginning would have been a lot simpler if they had listened, believed and obeyed. God didn't want them to have to deal with rotting food. He didn't plan the whole "provide food for My people" experience just to frustrate them. He told them how to handle His provision. Some of them chose to ignore Him.

Oh yes, sometimes we feel we know better than God what we need. We think our plans are so much wiser. We think that getting from Point A to Point B, C or D would be so much better if only God would do things our way. But God sees the end from the beginning. He knows everything that's going to happen along the way and He makes provision. Sometimes it might be that in His providing He wants us to learn to trust Him more. Just trust Him ... even when things get tough; even when His instructions don't make sense to us; even when we're scared. Trust and obey. There's no better way.

STOP COMPLAINING ABOUT EVERY LITTLE THING

The Israelites were great as long as there were no speed bumps on their journey. But the slightest sign of some kind of trauma and they quickly whined, complained and accused Moses of terrible things. They forgot that he was just the messenger and God was the leader. Their faith that God had orchestrated the changes leading to the new beginning for them was not very deep. Instead of seeing speed bumps as opportunities to see God's love and power at work, they wanted to give up. They actually wanted to go back to slavery in Egypt! That's even after God had done miracles to free them, protect them and provide water for them. They even recognized His awesome presence in the cloud that moved along with them.

The journey of life has ups and downs. There are good times and difficult times. There will be answered prayer and prayers still waiting for answers. There will be times filled with joy and times filled with fear. All of that is part of the incredible miracle of being alive. However, when you accept Christ as Savior and place your trust in Him, it has to be for all the times of life. Of course there will be fear once in a while and even worry or concern. You are human so allow yourself to feel. But don't dwell on the negative; take a deep breath and move toward trust instead of languishing in complaints and fear.

-HE GIVES-
power
TO THE WEAK;
strength
TO THE POWERLESS

ISAIAH 40:29

JERICHO
AND RAHAB

Based on Joshua 2, 6

JERICHO AND RAHAB
Joshua 2, 6

God chose Joshua to be the new leader of the Israelites after Moses died. He told Joshua that He was giving the Israelites the city of Jericho. So Joshua sent two spies into the city to see how hard it was going to be to take the city. They crept into the city and came to the house of the prostitute, Rahab. By then the king had heard there were spies in town. Rahab hid the two spies then asked them to protect her and her family when they came back to capture the city. They agreed to that.

Meanwhile God gave Joshua instructions for the way He wanted the Israelites to capture the city. He promised to be with Joshua and told him that the people would recognize Joshua as their new leader.

God told Joshua that for six days they should march all the way around the city in silence. Seven priests should march in front, carrying the Ark of the Covenant and other priests blew horns the whole time.

On the seventh day they marched around the city seven times. At the end of the seventh time the priests blew the horns and the people shouted! The great wall around Jericho fell down! Joshua and his army rushed in and captured the city! The found Rahab and her family and took them to safety, just as the spies had promised her.

RAHAB'S COURAGE

Joshua secretly sent two spies into Jericho to learn what the Israelites would be up against when they tried to capture the city. When the spies crept into Jericho they came to Rahab's house. She was a prostitute who didn't know God but there was something about what she knew of the Israelites' God that touched her heart. Rahab took a chance by hiding the spies. If the king found out what she had done, she could have been killed. Why would she take that risk? Simple. She did it because God had touched her heart. She believed that the Israelite God was the real God and that He could save her and give her a new start in life.

How courageous is your faith? Are you willing to risk your safety or even your life to honor God? Rahab did but when she hid the spies she didn't know if they would reciprocate her kindness. She didn't know if she could hide them from the soldiers. She truly took a chance. Faith that works only when life is easy is untested faith. How do you know how strong yours is if you never take the risk to trust God? Taking a chance is scary but Rahab did it when she was just a curious believer in God. She took a risk and God protected her and gave her a new beginning. Do you trust God enough to take a chance on Him?

ACCEPTING HELP FROM OTHERS

The people of Jericho feared the Israelites' strength because they knew God was fighting for them. They knew that He had guided them and performed miracles to protect them. Perhaps that fear is what made Rahab respect God and recognize that He is the only true God. When the spies came into Jericho she hid them and then made a deal with them because she knew she needed them to have help with her new beginning. She asked for help.

It's a hard thing for some people to ask for help. They like to feel they have things under control. They want to believe they don't need anyone else to help them. But, it's not a good idea to try to get through life on your own. God created us to live in community, in fact, He, Himself is community. Pay attention to the people God puts around you. He may have put them there just to help you move to your new beginning. Be willing to ask them for help or to accept their help when they offer.

This works the other way, too. Help others when you can to their new beginnings. When we allow others to be a part of our journey it bonds us together in friendship and purpose.

THE TAKING OF JERICHO

God told Joshua that He was giving him the city of Jericho. It was a done deal. Simple, right? Well, yes, but there were instructions that Joshua and his army had to follow. Their obedience played a role in their new beginning. God gave Joshua very specific instructions as to what the army should do leading up to the taking of Jericho and on the day when they would capture the city. His instructions made it clear that the city would fall because of His power, not because of the strength of the army.

It's exciting that God asks us to play a part in the changes or new beginnings He has for our lives by following Him in a specific way. It may not make sense to us at the time – the Israelites may have wondered about marching in silence around the city for six days, but they did it. There's no doubt that the residents of Jericho thought the Israelites were crazy. Now maybe that bothered the Israelites. Maybe Joshua's soldiers were afraid but they still did what he told them to do – what God had told him to do.

It's okay to be afraid as long as you keep obeying. It's okay if others think you're crazy, as long as you keep obeying. God will give you strength and perseverance to keep on keeping on and the result – a new beginning!

JOSHUA'S NEW DAY

"Today." God told Joshua, "Today I will begin to make you a great leader in the eyes of all the Israelites. They will know that I am with you, just as I was with Moses." (3:7) That day everything began to change for Joshua. He listened to God, he instructed the people and he led them to obey God's instructions. His life changed as the people began to accept him as God's chosen leader for them. When God told Joshua that this was the day, he didn't argue. He didn't say he couldn't do it or it was too hard. He just obeyed. Why? Well, he didn't argue with God but also he had the assurance that God would be with him every step of the way.

You wake up one day expecting it to be like any other day but then God says, "I have something new for you today." Of course everything can change in a moment. But instead of running with the new thing, do you waste time looking backward at what used to be? Do you question whether God meant this new thing for you or did you intercept someone else's instructions?

Change can be disorienting and even more so when it comes quickly. But, if Joshua had doubted that he could do the job God told him to do or if he had argued with God or looked back instead of stepping into the new – history would be a lot different – his and Israel's!

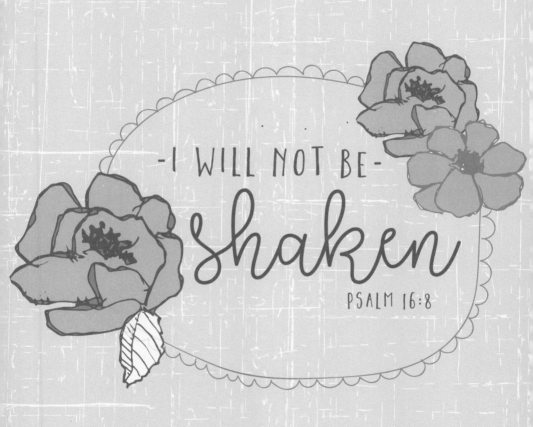

-I WILL NOT BE-

shaken

PSALM 16:8

DEBORAH

Based on Judges 4-5

DEBORAH
Judges 4-5

Each time the Israelites disobeyed God they were captured by another nation and oppressed. They cried out to God for help, and as He always did, He helped them. God told the judge, Deborah, what needed to be done to gain their freedom. He told her to have Barak gather 10,000 warriors to fight. God would send the commander of the enemy army, Sisera to fight Barak and God would give Barak the victory and the Israelites would be free.

Barak listened to Deborah's instructions from God and said, "Yes, I will do what you say God is instructing me to do but only if you will go with me."

Deborah answered, "OK, I will go with you but then the honor of defeating Sisera will go to a woman and not to you." The two armies met up near Mount Tabor and when Barak's 10,000 soldiers attacked Sisera's army of 900 chariots they were thrown into a panic. Sisera jumped down from his chariot and ran. Barak's army killed every one of Sisera's soldiers.

Sisera ran to the tent of a woman named Jael. He told her to tell him if anyone came looking for him then he laid down to rest. When he fell asleep, Jael picked up a stake and hammered it through his head, killing him. That day the Israelites knew that God had defeated their enemy again!

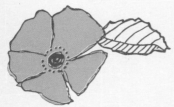

DEBORAH GAVE A SHOUT

Deborah was one of the few female judges in Israel's history. She listened to the Israelites' problems and gave advice to solve them. She listened to God so her advice was wise and God-centered. When God heard the Israelite's cry for help He told Deborah to give a shout out to Barak to lead his army to win their freedom. Deborah did what God asked her to do ... Barak did not. For whatever reason he would not do the job by himself. So Deborah changed the plan. Maybe God whispered to her, "OK, you go with him." Maybe she made the call on her own because she knew that God wanted His people freed.

Deborah warned Barak that he would not get the honor of defeating the enemy. That honor would go to a woman. Barak didn't seem to care. The battle was won and God's people were freed because Deborah changed the plans and then stepped up to give Barak the strength he needed to do the job.

Sometimes the way you expect things to happen has to change and you must get creative in order to accomplish what must happen. It takes thinking outside the box. It takes a closeness to God so that you know His heart.

THE WOMAN IN THE TENT

Barak didn't feel he could lead the battle against the Israelites' enemies by himself. Deborah warned him that he would not then have
the honor of defeating the Canaanites. That honor would then go
to a woman. Of course that could be interpreted as Deborah getting
the honor and we certainly know her name. But, there was another
woman in the story, just an average woman who was hanging out
in her tent. That day Jael became something more. Her name is re-
corded in Scripture because she killed Sisera, the commander of the
Canaanite army.

Being in the right place at the right time may bring opportunities
to be the instigator of change for yourself and a whole bunch of
other people. Jael may not have known all that had gone on between
Deborah and Barak, but she knew Sisera and she knew what she had
to do when she had the chance. She knew who her enemy was. She
knew God wanted His people free. She made the choice to be the
instrument to make that change happen.

Pay attention to what's going on around you. Know the situation and
be in the moment. God may use you to bring incredible change!

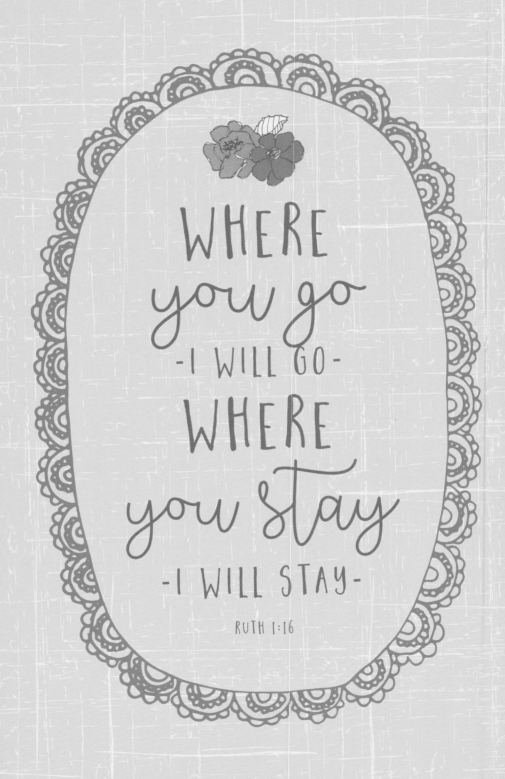

WHERE
you go
-I WILL GO-
WHERE
you stay
-I WILL STAY-

RUTH 1:16

RUTH AND NAOMI

based on the book of Ruth

RUTH AND NAOMI
The Book of Ruth

Naomi and Elimelech escaped the famine in Judah by taking their sons, Mahlon and Kilion to live in Moab. But they weren't there too long before Elimelech died, leaving Naomi with her two sons. The boys grew up and each married Moabite women. Their names were Ruth and Orpah. Then, Naomi's sons both died. Three women … alone … no one to support them.

When Naomi heard that the famine was over in Judah she decided to go home. Both of her daughters-in-law wanted to go with her. But Naomi told them to stay home with their families. She thought they should stay in Moab and find new husbands. Orpah decided that was a good idea and she went home but Ruth firmly declared that she wanted to go with Naomi. She wanted to be part of Naomi's family and worship Naomi's God. So Ruth left her family and her country behind and set off for Bethlehem with Naomi.

Family and friends welcomed Naomi home, but she told them to call her Mara, which means bitter because God had allowed such cruelty in her life. The two women had no way to provide for themselves so Ruth began following workers in a field and picking up grain they dropped so she and Naomi could make bread. The owner of the field, Boaz, liked Ruth and was kind to her. Naomi encouraged Ruth to get to know him. Eventually Ruth and Boaz were married and they had a son, Obed, who became the grandfather of King David and was in the ancestral line of Jesus!

UNPLANNED, UNEXPECTED CHANGE

Maybe you've been there ... your life has settled into a smooth zone. Job is going well. Kids are doing fine. You've even reached a place of financial comfort. You're starting to relax ... then suddenly the bottom falls out with a job loss or a marriage ends or illness ... something that leaves you in an unexpected situation which leads to scary stress — financially, relationally, emotionally. *All 3 happened in Sept. — Oct. til now Nov. 2021*

Change. Yeah, it's no fun. Change is what happened to Elimelech and Naomi. The bottom fell out of their normal life and to survive they had to move to another country. It couldn't have been easy. They left everything familiar — home, family, work, friends and those who worshiped their God. Scary stuff. Did they trust that God would take care of them, no matter what? They apparently did. Their faith in God was basic to their lives. We see that later in Naomi's life.

Unplanned change can knock you to the ground. But, do you stay there or pick yourself up and look for the blessing of the "next"? Change does not mean the end, it just means change, God always has a next, And ... it's always pretty good.

THEY'RE WATCHING

Did Naomi wonder why? Did she grow weary of trusting? When her sons died, did she wonder where God was? Did she struggle to stay strong in her faith? Yes, it appears she did. When she got back to Bethlehem she even told people to call her "Bitter" instead of Naomi because God had allowed such cruelty in her life. Naomi was human. She was a wife and mother. She was far from home and family. She surely grieved her family.

However much Naomi struggled, she never gave up on God. As much as she hurt, she kept stretching her arms up to him. Naomi probably wasn't thinking about whether anyone was watching the realness of her faith, she was just trying to get through the pain. But, Ruth was watching and what she learned changed her life.

The fact is you never know who's watching. You never know what someone is learning by watching how you live your faith through problems. Your willingness to share your struggle and your God-honoring questions, uncertainty and pain may speak to another person's heart and move them to faith in God. Live your faith honestly ... in good times and hard times.

TOUGH DECISIONS

When Naomi decided to go home to Bethlehem, she told her daughters-in-law to go back home to their families. That made sense. She knew she was going to have trouble providing for herself, let alone take care of them, too. They were still young women so their families could arrange other marriages for them and they could have children, in other words, have the expected normal life for a woman of their time. Yes, it made sense. Maybe Orpah was the sensible one because she took Naomi's advice, hugged her mother-in-law goodbye and went home.

However, Ruth refused to go home. She chose to leave her family and everything familiar in order to go with Naomi. That couldn't have been an easy decision.

Sometimes the choices before you are confusing. It may be hard to know which is the right one because, frankly, the right choice is often the hardest one. It may be the one that means leaving loved ones, a familiar place or job or even ending a relationship. The right choice means looking at the big picture and not the minutiae of today. Ruth made the right choice and God's blessings filled her life.

STEPPING UP!

Naomi and Ruth made the long trip to Bethlehem from Moab. But when they arrived, they had no idea how they were going to survive. How would they get food? They were women and they didn't have jobs. Ruth saw the need. She knew that caring for Naomi was her job so she found a way to do so. It wasn't pretty. It wasn't influential. It wasn't a lot. But they survived.

Ruth saw a need. She stepped up to fill it. Was it easy? Probably not. Was she treated badly? Perhaps. Did it stop her? No.

Ruth is known for her loyalty to Naomi but her strength and courage are also worthy of noting. Ruth committed to go with Naomi. She committed to follow God. So when a need faced her, she committed to fill it and God blessed her greatly for her willingness.

Filling needs isn't easy. It may not be something you really want to do but you will never know how God might bless you through your service if you walk away from the challenge. Step up and see God bless!

GOD'S BIG PLAN

Recap of the story: Ruth and Elimelech left their home in Bethlehem and moved to Moab. Their sons married Moabite girls who did not share their faith. Elimelech died. Both of Naomi's sons died. Naomi was left with two Moabite daughters-in-law. She decided to go home when the famine in Bethlehem ended. Daughter-in-law Ruth insisted on going with her. Ruth worked hard to provide for them. She met Boaz who owned the field where she picked up grain. Boaz and Ruth married. Ruth had a son who became the grandfather of King David and ... Jesus. Ruth is a woman mentioned in Jesus' line of ancestry.

Of course Naomi had no idea of what the big picture would be from her pain and loss. But she trusted God and even though she grieved her losses, she believed he had a bigger plan than the pain of the moment.

Don't get stuck in the pain of the moment, trust that God has a bigger plan and that it will be good. The pain of crises may lead to blessings you can barely imagine. It will surely take you to deeper faith and dependence on God. That's the biggest blessing of all.

Be still
-BEFORE THE LORD-
AND
wait
patiently
-FOR HIM-
PSALM 37:7

HANNAH'S PAIN

Based on 1 Samuel 1

HANNAH'S PAIN
I Samuel I

Elkanah had two wives. Peninnah had children but Hannah did not. Hannah was sad about not having children. When Elkanah made a sacrifice at the temple he gave Peninnah a double portion of the meat because she had children. Hannah got only one portion since she had no children. Of course Peninnah took this as an opportunity to make even more fun of Hannah than usual. Hannah got so upset that she wouldn't even eat. Elkanah tried to comfort her. He wanted her to be happy just to be his wife.

But Hannah wanted a child. The next time they went to the temple to worship, Hannah went in by herself. She fell down on her knees and cried out to God, begging Him for a child. She even promised that if He would give her a son she would give her boy back to God, to serve Him. Eli, the priest saw her on the floor crying and he thought she had been drinking. She explained that she was simply crying out to God.

"Then, go on home," Eli said. "God has heard your prayer. He will grant your request." Hannah thanked him, went home and began to eat again.

Sure enough by the next year, Hannah had a son. She named him Samuel which means, "I asked the Lord for him." Hannah remembered her promise to God and when Samuel was old enough Hannah took him to the temple to live with Eli and learn how to serve God.

HANNAH'S PRAYER

Hannah took the best course of action in order to change her situation. Things in her life were not the way she wanted them to be but instead of taking some course of action that would not be honoring to God or her husband, she prayed. She prayed hard. She laid it all out before God. In fact she laid it all out with such deep heartfelt emotion that Eli thought she had come to the temple drunk. Did Hannah know the priest would hear her crying out to God? Maybe she was so filled with yearning for a child that she didn't even care if another person heard her.

Admitting and revealing deep, honest emotion is not easy and of course, not always appropriate to share with other people. But, it is always appropriate and honest to share with God. If you long for your situation to change — whether it's to be married, have a child, change jobs, make a friend — whatever it is ... talk to Him about it. He is the author of new beginnings and ... He loves you!

HANNAH PRAYED AND BELIEVED

Hannah was so upset because she didn't have a child that she wouldn't eat. Not even her husband's comforting words helped her feel better. Nothing would fill the pain in her heart except becoming a mother. But once Eli, the priest said, "May God grant your request," Hannah felt better. She seemed to believe that everything would be alright. She went home and ate.

Have you ever been so distraught that you couldn't eat? Maybe food didn't taste good or you were so upset that eating actually made you ill. But then if you don't eat for a while, you get physically run down and can even actually get sick.

What's interesting about this story is that Hannah ate. She must have believed so certainly that God would answer her prayer that she went home and resumed normal activity. She prayed "in faith, believing" which is exactly how Scripture tells you to pray.

Does this mean that God will give you all you ask Him to do? No, because He sees a bigger picture than you do. He knows what is best for you. But you can pray, believing that He hears and believing that He will do what is best because He loves you very much.

HONORING GOD FOR HONORING YOU

Hannah knew where the answer to her prayer came from and she gave God the credit for the precious baby boy she had. The meaning of names was quite important in Old Testament times and Samuel's name means, "I asked the Lord for him." So, yes, Hannah honored God's gift to her. What else did Hannah do? She kept her promise to God.

Hannah prayed passionately asking God to give her a child. She promised that if He gave her a son she would give her son back to God to serve Him. Do you wonder if Hannah was tempted to push that promise to the fringes of her life? Do you wonder if she longed to keep her little boy close to her? That might seem likely, but Hannah did not do that. She honored her promise to God because He honored her prayer.

Good lesson there. Honor God, even when it's hard. Even when the change that's required by honoring Him might be difficult. Honor Him for honoring you by hearing your prayer, answering your prayer and giving you new beginnings.

-TRUST IN THE-

Lord

WITH ALL YOUR

heart

AND DO NOT LEAN

-ON YOUR OWN-

UNDERSTANDING

PROVERBS 3:5

ELIJAH AND BREAD FOR THE WIDOW

Based on 1 Kings 17:8-16

ELIJAH AND BREAD FOR A WIDOW
I Kings 17:8-16

Elijah was hungry. So, God told him to go to Zarephath. God had arranged for a widow woman there to provide food for him. When he got to the town, Elijah saw a woman picking up sticks to make a fire. He asked her for a cup of water and as she was going to get it, he added, "And bring me some bread, too, please."

The woman sadly said, "The truth is that I do not have even a slice of bread in the house. All I have is a tiny bit of flour. In fact I was gathering these sticks to make a fire to bake one tiny loaf of bread for my son and I. After that last meal we will die."

"OK, don't worry. Just go ahead and make the bread but make just a small loaf for me first," Elijah said, "Then use the flour and oil that's left to make food for you and your son. God promises that there will always be flour and oil for you until the drought is over here and food is plentiful again."

The woman didn't question Elijah at all. She just did what he said. Sure enough, there was flour and oil to make bread for as long as they needed it. She and her son had all the food they needed.

BASIC NEEDS

God had already taken care of Elijah in miraculous ways. He sent birds to bring Elijah food! Now, He had a new plan for Elijah's care that would also take care of a widow woman and her son who would soon starve to death without His intervention.

God provided a very basic need for Elijah ... food. Basic. Necessary. If you've ever been without a basic need (as Elijah was) or feared that you would be then you realize that God's daily provisions for you affect every day of your life. Each day is a new beginning and a new opportunity to notice how God provides. Do you remember to appreciate those very basic gifts of food, water, rest, love, friendships, His Word, prayer, His presence, answered prayer and on and on.

An awareness of the ways God cares for you each day will remind you of His constant presence and moment-by-moment love and care for you.

WIDOW'S FAITH

The widow woman may seem to be incidental to this story but she most certainly is not. She was facing starvation and watching her son starve to death. Things looked very hopeless for her. Then the man of God comes along and asks her to share some of her last little bit of food, promising that God would provide for her and her son. She could have been selfish and refused to share with Elijah. She could have declared that every bit of that food was necessary for her and her son. But she didn't. She trusted the man of God. She trusted God. And her new beginning was one of life!

Sometimes the things God asks you to do may seem confusing or even pointless. Like the widow's situation it can look like you would be moving backward by doing what He says. It may look as though you are defeating the ultimate goal you are pursuing. Sometimes God takes you through dark places where all you can do is depend on Him but He never abandons you. He has a plan and your trust and obedience takes you to the new beginning you desire – just as the widow's obedience did for her and her son.

perhaps

-YOU WERE MADE QUEEN-

FOR SUCH A *time*

-AS THIS-

ESTHER 4:14

QUEEN ESTHER

Based on the book
of Esther

QUEEN ESTHER
The Book of Esther •

King Xerxes needed a queen so a contest was held. Beautiful girls were brought to the palace and Esther was made queen. She was a Jewish girl, encouraged by her cousin Mordecai to enter the contest and to keep her Jewishness a secret.

One day Mordecai heard two guards plotting to kill the king. He told Queen Esther and she told the king. Mordecai saved the king's life.

Haman was a powerful man in the kingdom. Everyone except Mordecai bowed down when he passed by. Haman was so angry that he got the king's permission to kill all the Jews in the land. He also built a pole to impale Mordecai.

Mordecai told Esther of Haman's plan and begged her to ask the king to save her people. Esther could be killed just for going to the king without being called. But she invited the king and Haman to a dinner. She didn't mention Haman's plan at all that night but invited them to a second dinner.

One night the king couldn't sleep so he read the book of history of his reign of when Mordecai saved his life. He decided to honor Mordecai. The next day the king asked Haman what should be done for a man the king wanted to honor. He even had Haman carry out the honor for Mordecai.

At the second dinner Queen Esther told the king of Haman's plan to kill the Jews and that it would include her since she was Jewish. The king was angry and had Haman hanged on the same pole Haman had intended to use to kill Mordecai. The Israelites were saved because of Queen Esther's courage!

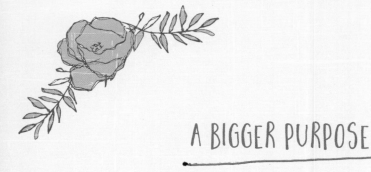

A BIGGER PURPOSE

How awesome is Esther's story? She was just an oppressed Jewish girl ... albeit a beautiful Jewish girl who was whisked from obscurity to royalty! That's the stuff dreams are made of, right? Yes, except this huge change in Esther's life came with a responsibility and purpose ... to save her people.

Did Esther know the purpose in her new beginning in the beginning? No. Did she question her position in doing it? Yes, at first. After all, the easy thing would have been to say, "Look, Mordecai, I'm the queen but my husband could have me killed just for entering his presence without being called. So, I'm really sorry about the plight of our people, but I can't really help." But Esther didn't do that. She asked for prayer. She fasted. She faced into the task.

 Pay attention to the possible "Whys" of your new beginnings or changes in life. Notice if there is a bigger purpose than just what happens with you. Face into the task with God's guidance and strength and a prayer army supporting you.

LISTEN TO THE MORDECAI IN YOUR WORLD

It was Mordecai's idea for Esther to enter the contest to become queen. It was at Mordecai's urging that Esther interceded with the king to stop Haman's plans to destroy the Jews. Mordecai was instrumental in this new beginning for Esther. He motivated her, encouraged her and he challenged her to do the job before her. Did Mordecai know the dangers that Esther would face? Possibly. He sure knew that Haman was not a nice guy. He knew that his people needed an advocate. Perhaps he believed Esther was the answer.

Esther was instrumental in saving her people but she may never have had the opportunity if not for Mordecai. Maybe there's someone in your life who is pushing you to something that looks like a job too big for you or maybe it looks dangerous so you're frightened. If your encourager loves and honors God and walks closely with Him, trust his or her heart. Pay attention to how God is using that person in your life. God has given them an important job, too, and he or she pushes you to do the job God has planned for you.

MORDECAI HONORED FOR HONORING THE KING

Mordecai was Esther's encourager and he challenged her to take a risk with her own life to save the Jewish people, which, of course, included him. But he got an even more specific new beginning in this story. He was the victim of Haman's anger due to his refusal to bow down to the arrogant man. Haman even had a special gallows built on which to hang Mordecai. He wanted Mordecai gone!

What saved Mordecai? Something good he had done years before came to the king's attention and he decided to protect Mordecai from Haman's evil plan.

Mordecai's new beginning came from good choices he had made previously. He was honored for saving the king's life years before. When he did that, he didn't know how important that was going to be in his future. Perhaps he even wondered if he shouldn't have received some sort of commendation at the time and was possibly even disappointed that his good deed went unnoticed. But ... nothing is wasted with God. Nothing. Honor Him. Live for Him. Obey Him. Serve Him. He notices. He will reward in His timing.

HAVING A PLAN

Esther's story is not the first time that God used the courage and bravery of one person to save an entire nation. It's not the first time a woman risked her own life to fulfill God's plan. God uses people ... individuals willing to serve Him. He uses those who hold nothing back from Him, not even their lives.

Mordecai made Haman angry by refusing to bow down to him. For revenge, Haman planned to get rid of not just Mordecai, but all the Jews! Word of Haman's plans leaked to Mordecai so he knew the situation was serious. Esther was the answer. He even told her that perhaps she had become queen for just "such a time as this."

Think about what Esther did — she dared to enter the king's presence without being summoned; she invited the king and Haman to dinner TWICE; she waited for the right moment to reveal Haman's wicked plan and reveal her own ethnicity; she asked the king to save her people.

Esther had a plan. She had the prayer support of her people. She was methodical and intentional in doing the job before her and as a result the nation of Israel was saved!

-YOU ARE THE GOD WHO WORKS-

wonders

PSALM 77:14

ELIZABETH AND ZECHARIAH

Based on Luke 1

ELIZABETH AND ZECHARIAH
Luke I

Zechariah and Elizabeth had no children. They had always wanted to be parents but Elizabeth had never been able to conceive. Now they were old and the prospect of having a baby seemed preposterous.

Zechariah was a priest and one day he was serving in the temple. He was chosen to be the lone priest who went into the inner sanctuary to burn incense. A large crowd of people stood outside praying while Zechariah was alone in there. While he was in there an angel appeared to Zechariah. The angel told him that God had heard his and Elizabeth's prayers for a child. "Your wife will have a son and you shall name him John," the angel said. "He will be filled with the Holy Spirit and will bring people to God."

Zechariah thought that was amazing news. "How can I be sure this is true?" he asked.

The angel said that since he didn't believe God's news, Zechariah wouldn't be able to speak until the baby was born.

Sure enough, he couldn't utter a word until Elizabeth gave birth and he scratched out on a tablet, "The baby's name is John."

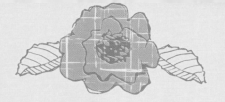

GOD'S TIMING

Zechariah and Elizabeth waited a long time for God to bring them the change in their lives that they longed for – the experience of parenthood. No doubt Elizabeth and Zechariah felt sadness at times as they longed to be parents. However, it was necessary for them to wait for God's timing and stay faithful to Him as they waited. Imagine their joy, as they were old enough to be grandparents when they first became parents. They knew without a doubt that God had heard their prayers and answered them in His perfect timing. The timing of the change in their lives was directly related to the birth of Jesus – God had a plan.

Waiting is hard, isn't it? Of course you know in your mind that God's timing is always best but when you're longing for something particular, waiting is hard. Even if you see later that God was waiting to make the change in your life in order to coincide with something else, it's hard. And you may not see that evidence for years and years, if ever.

Waiting for God's timing builds deeper trust in Him and belief in the assurance that He has things under control. He knows exactly the right time to bring change and new beginnings to your life.

ELIZABETH'S DISGRACE

It was a big deal in Elizabeth's time for a woman to be childless. It was a disgrace that she lived with every day. God's new beginning for her gave her identity with other mothers and the fulfillment of that experience. She also had the blessing of understanding that this baby was a specific gift from God and that God had a specific purpose for her boy. She surely must have realized the blessing of waiting for God's timing. Were her years of disgrace difficult? No doubt. Was she sad? More than likely. Was it all worth it in the end? Given Elizabeth's faith in God ... absolutely.

So maybe you're going through a hard time and you keep praying for God to bring it to an end. You just know that with one little sweep of His godly hand He could make everything better ... but He doesn't do it. It's hard to understand and maybe you wonder if He even knows how much you're hurting. He does. He also knows that it's in the painful times when you are hurting that your faith will grow deeper because you having no one to turn to except Him. Trust Him to walk through dark times with you.

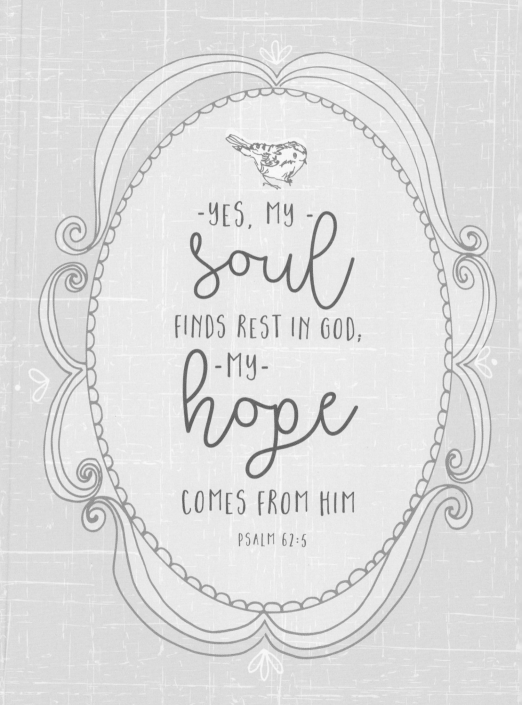

-YES, MY-

soul

FINDS REST IN GOD;

-MY-

hope

COMES FROM HIM

PSALM 62:5

ANNOUNCEMENT OF JESUS

Based on Matthew 1:18-25;
Luke 1:26-56

ANNOUNCEMENT OF JESUS
Matthew 1:18-25; Luke 1:26-56

God pays attention and He noticed Mary. She was just a teenage girl who sought in her heart to honor and obey God. She loved Him. God noticed and specifically chose her for the honor of being Jesus' earthly mother. The angel Gabriel came to Mary and told her that God had chosen her to be the mother of His Son whom she should name Jesus. Mary questioned the angel but when He assured her that God had chosen her, she responded with, "I am the Lord's servant. Let everything happen just as you have said."

The angel Gabriel also appeared to Joseph who was engaged to marry Mary. He warned him that Mary was pregnant and that people would talk because Mary was already pregnant but the child was God's child, not another man's child. The angel told Joseph that it was OK to go ahead and marry her. Joseph listened to the angel and he did marry her. They became the earthly parents of the very holy Jesus.

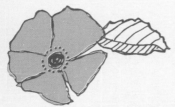

DIFFICULT TIMES WITH BLESSINGS AHEAD

God asked Mary to do something difficult. She was an unmarried, betrothed teenage girl and He asked her to let Him make her pregnant. Wow, that's a huge change for a young girl to process. She had to expect there would be gossip. She may have been accused of disgracing her family. She certainly could have expected her fiancé to walk away from her ... but God, whom she loved and served asked her to have a baby – His Son – who would be the Messiah that the whole world was holding its breath for as it expected Him to come.

Mary said yes to the difficult task and her world was instantly changed. Mary walked closely enough with God to trust that this change was good – for her and for all mankind.

Are you facing changes that look dark and ominous to you? Can you not see a bright light ahead? Do you believe God is walking with you, guiding your steps? Then trust Him to get you through this time. Trust that He has a purpose in it that will ultimately bring blessings greater than you can even imagine.

WHY DID GOD CHOOSE MARY?

Why did God choose Mary to be the mother of His Son? She was just a child by today's standards. She hadn't really lived yet. She had little life experience under her belt. It proves a point that God looked at Mary's heart and saw that she was devoted to Him. She loved Him, was submitted to Him, trusted Him completely. What a blessing that He recognized that devotion in her.

Mary's new beginning didn't come because she "acted" devoted. She wasn't trying to impress anyone or pretend to be something she wasn't. God wouldn't be fooled by her dramatic skills. She wasn't chosen because she did the right thing because she knew she was supposed to do it. She was chosen because God saw that in her heart she desired to honor and obey Him. Was she perfect all the time? Of course not. But what He saw in her heart was all He needed.

Where is your heart? Are you living for God out of habit or for appearances' sake when your heart is somewhere else? Submit your heart to Him. Confess your sins and repent of them. Then seek His new beginnings in your life.

THE WORDS OF OTHERS

Joseph is an interesting character in this story. He must have been well respected and also a man who obeyed God; apparent since God knew that he would be the earthly father caring for Jesus.

Once it became obvious to the community that Mary was carrying a child, Joseph may have been the object of snide comments, about her faithfulness to him. It couldn't have been easy. Did he tell the story of the angel's visit? Did he quickly respond to criticism with, "No, wait! This baby is the child of God. He's the Messiah!" We don't know what Joseph said or did except that he proceeded with the commitment to marry his fiancée and to raise and protect this special Child.

Joseph's new beginning may have brought difficult times because of others but he worked through that, honoring God, Mary and Jesus.

There will always be the naysayers. There will always be jealous critics. There will always be negative people. But if you are certain that God has opened a door for you, go in, appreciate the new beginning, follow Him and ignore those who don't really know what they are talking about anyway.

believe
-IN POSSIBILITIES-
WITH GOD
all things
-ARE POSSIBLE-

MATTHEW 19:26

WOMAN
AT THE WELL

Based on John 4:1-26

WOMAN AT THE WELL
John 4:1-26

Jesus and His disciples were on their way to Galilee and they passed through Samaria. Around noon they stopped by Jacob's well and the disciples went to get food. While Jesus was resting there a woman came to get water. "Could I have a drink?" He asked her. The woman was stunned that a Jew would speak to her since Jews and Samaritans didn't like each other. But Jesus told her that if she knew who He was she would ask Him for the living water He could give because with that water she would never be thirsty again. It would give her eternal life.

The woman eagerly asked for His water. When He told her to get her husband she had to answer that she didn't have a husband. Jesus knew she had been married five times but wasn't married to the man she was living with currently. When she called Him a prophet and tried to talk about the different beliefs of the Jews and Samaritans Jesus wasn't sidetracked. He said that one day everyone would worship God in spirit and in truth. "It will all make sense when the Messiah comes," she answered.

"I am He," Jesus said. The woman instantly believed Him and raced back to town, calling everyone to come meet the Messiah! Crowds of people came rushing to see Him. Many people believed that day.

Meanwhile Jesus' disciples returned with food but He wouldn't eat. They didn't understand. They knew He must be hungry. But Jesus told them that His nourishment came from doing God's will.

DEFENSIVE WOMAN

The Samaritan woman had not had an easy life. For whatever reason she had bounced from marriage to marriage and apparently had now given up on marriage altogether. She knew that Jews considered themselves above Samaritans so she started this conversation with Jesus from a defensive point. She was probably used to being defensive because she had been beaten down for so long. She felt she had nothing positive to offer. Her self-image was too low to retrieve. Jesus calmly explained to her that He was the Messiah she was waiting for and … she believed Him. Her belief brought a new beginning of life with God for eternity.

It can be hard to recover from a life that hasn't been easy. If you've been beaten down day after day, year after year then it may be difficult to believe in yourself and to believe that you deserve anything good. Maybe, like the woman at the well, you are hungering for truth or longing for connection. Can you, like the woman at the well, hear Jesus' words and know they are for you. Can you believe that He is the Messiah and that His love is for you? Yes? Then you have a new beginning!

NO RESPECT

The people of Sychar may not have held the woman Jesus spoke with at the well in very high regard. She may have been considered a loose woman due to all her marriages and her current relationship situation. It's suspect that she went to the well during the hot part of the day rather than in the cooler morning time. Either she didn't want to be around the other women or she knew they didn't want to be around her.

So, why did they listen to her and go to check out the man at the well?

There must have been something in her face, in her eyes, in the way she spoke. She was different so they listened and they checked out the Man at the well ... and they believed, too. Their lives were changed because they paid attention to someone they had more than likely always dismissed without a thought.

Do you think the people around you don't pay any attention to you? Does your own self-image hamper how you interact with others? Yet, you know the truth of God's love and salvation. You have the knowledge that can change their lives. Like the woman at the well, share that news with certainty, energy and passion.

DON'T BE AFRAID

-JUST-

believe

MARK 5:36

JAIRUS AND HIS DAUGHTER

Based on Mark 5:22-43

JAIRUS AND HIS DAUGHTER
Mark 5:22-43

Jairus was a leader in the synagogue. He was a devout Jew and while his colleagues may not have believed that Jesus was the Messiah, Jairus had heard some things that at least convinced him that Jesus was someone special. So when Jairus' 12 year-old daughter got very sick he went right to Jesus. He believed that Jesus could make his beloved daughter well so he asked Him to come home right away with him. Jesus started to go but then another emergency interrupted him. It must have been difficult for Jairus to wait while Jesus handled the other situation.

Just as Jesus was ready to go with Jairus, servants from his home arrived to tell him that his daughter had already died so he shouldn't bother Jesus any further.

Jesus turned to Jairus and said, "Don't be afraid. Have faith." He called Peter, James and John to come with Him and went to Jairus' house. It was filled with people sobbing and grieving for the death of the little girl. Jesus told them to stop because she was only sleeping. They laughed at Him but He ignored them and sent everyone out of the house except Jairus, his wife and Peter, James and John. Then He took the little girl's hand and said, "Get up." She did! She was alive again and her parents rejoiced!

JAIRUS' PRAYER ANSWERED

Jairus believed and he "prayed." Of course he could pray in person to Jesus — face to face — but he DID pray. His prayer was answered, in Jesus' time and because Jairus believed. He didn't waver. He prayed in faith believing and Jesus answered.

Do you pray for changes to come in your life? Do you believe that God will answer your prayer? Really believe? Scripture says to pray "in faith, believing." It says that a person who prays and doubts is like a wave of the sea, blown and tossed by the wind. If that's how you pray, you have a problem.

Do you look for change in your life and hope for new beginnings? Pray and ask God for His guidance and help. Believe that He will answer. Trust His guidance and don't be afraid to start moving forward. If you're moving in the wrong direction, trust Him to stop you. If you're moving forward and you are afraid, trust Him to strengthen you and walk with you. Be courageous in your asking as Jairus was and patient in the answer coming, as Jairus was.

JAIRUS' DAUGHTER IS HEALED

The sick girl was only 12 years old and she was very sick. Even if she knew who Jesus was, she was unable to go to Him for help. Her dad interceded for her. He "prayed" for her. He asked Jesus to come heal his girl. His faith was rewarded and the little girl was given a new beginning. The change in her life was a reward for the faith of her father. She probably celebrated Jesus' love and power big time once she was back on her feet! She probably thanked her dad for his faithful intervention, too.

You are not meant to go through this life alone. God puts people in your life to help you, mentor you, encourage you and intercede for you. You're not in this life alone. So, when you're going through difficult times and you need help, pray for yourself, but also enlist the powerful prayers of those around you. Share your life with them. Celebrate the changes and new beginnings that come into your life with those who have prayed for you and loved you.

BYSTANDERS!

Peter James, John, Jairus and his wife were allowed into the room when Jesus raised the little girl back to life. They knew the little girl was dead. They saw Jesus take her hand and say, "Get up, little girl." They saw her get up! They heard Jesus say, "Give her something to eat." Amazing miracle and those five people got to witness it. When a person goes through a dark time and sees God intervene, faith grows stronger.

Why did Jesus allow those bystanders to witness this miracle? Perhaps He knew that witnessing something so incredibly miraculous would kick their faith into high gear. He knew they would never be the same.

Have you ever seen something happen in your life that is so amazing, so unexplainable that you know it could only be God? Did your faith grow stronger? When you've been through something painful or scary and you see God intervene and you know it could only be Him … your heart opens a bit wider and your trust grows a bit deeper and you know that He loves you. That's a change in your walk with Him because it grows deeper and stronger.

blessed
-IS SHE WHO HAS-
believed
THE LORD WILL FULFILL
-HIS-
promises TO HER

LUKE 1:45

WOMAN WITH THE
ISSUE OF BLOOD

Based on Mark 5:25-34

WOMAN WITH THE ISSUE OF BLOOD
Mark 5:25-34

We don't even know her name. She had been bleeding for 12 years. She had been to doctor after doctor and while they gladly took her money none of them helped her. She was tired, scared, broke and literally at the end of her rope. She had heard of Jesus. She knew He healed sick people. He taught about God. He seemed to be kind and concerned about people. She also knew that He was surrounded by a crowd of people wherever He went. So she came up with a plan. She joined the crowd following along behind Jesus. It was crowded and noisy. Everyone seemed to want something from Him.

A temple leader stopped Jesus and asked Him to come home with him to help his sick daughter. That was her chance. She fell to her knees and stretched her arm through the crowd until she touched the hem of Jesus' robe. She knew ... she believed that just touching his robe would heal her! Instantly the bleeding stopped. She was healed!

But then Jesus stopped talking to the temple leader and asked, "Who touched Me?" She was caught! She courageously stood up and admitted that it was her and that she thought just touching the hem of Jesus' robe would heal her.

Jesus said, "Your faith has made you well. Go in peace." She was healed because of her faith.

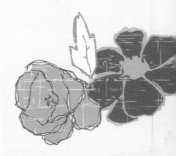

DEEPEST FAITH

For twelve years this woman had lived with the problem that rendered her unclean. She must have felt lonely, scared and hopeless until she heard Jesus was coming to town. Perhaps her courage at joining the crowd was unwelcome; perhaps no one wanted her to be around them; undoubtedly there were many people clamoring for Jesus' attention and wanting Him to do things for them. She was strong. She saw her opportunity and took it. Her courage came from her faith that Jesus could heal her. What's even more amazing is that she was so certain of His healing power that she believed just touching the hem of His garment would heal her. That's amazing faith. Her faith was rewarded with healing.

Deep faith gave this woman the change she longed for. How's your faith? Is it strong enough to believe Jesus wouldn't need to speak healing words or touch you at all? Is it strong enough to believe that touching His robe would be enough? That's a depth of faith that doesn't fit in our "Me First and Only" world where we desire personal and exclusive attention. However, it's a faith strong enough to put God first!

WITNESSING A MIRACLE

Wonder what the crowd thought when they realized this woman was there among them?

Lots of people hung around Jesus. Some may have been curious about His teachings. Many probably wanted to see miracles or have Him do miracles for them. They were there for the extreme. So what happened to them when they actually SAW a miracle? Did it change them?

They saw a woman who had extreme faith and if they were following Jesus just for the "show" did it make them stop and think about who He is when they saw the miracle of healing from when she just touched cloth? Did seeing her extreme faith and Jesus' compassion change them? Would it change you?

Step back for a moment and stop focusing on what God does for you. Look around at what He does for others. See His faithful, compassionate love. Remember there are millions of people calling out to Him every moment. Remember that even as He answers your prayers, He is doing so from the perspective of a much bigger picture and much more focused purpose than your requests reflect. Trust Him to do what's best for you. Let His love and compassion change you.

-SHE CONFIDENTLY-
trusts THE LORD
TO TAKE
care of her

PSALM 112:7

WIDOW'S OFFERING

Based on Mark 12:41-44

WIDOW'S OFFERING
Mark 12:41-44

Jesus was in the temple and He saw different people giving their offerings. They each approached the offering box and dropped in their offering. He noticed a woman who came forward. She was a widow and was obviously quite poor. Jesus saw her drop two coins into the box. That wasn't much – the two coins together were worth just a fraction of a penny. He also saw some people who were well dressed and obviously quite wealthy come forward to give their offerings. They gave large amounts of money.

Jesus turned to His disciples and said, "That widow woman who only gave two small coins has given a greater offering than the rich people who gave more money. She gave all she had. The rich people gave their extra money. They have more than enough left to live on. She gave all. They gave some."

TOTAL TRUST

The poverty-stricken woman in this story held nothing back from God. The sacrificial gift she gave was reflective of a humble heart completely devoted to God and fully trusting Him to meet her needs. She apparently had a good understanding of the bigger picture of what's important — not gathering more and more wealth and stuff — but caring for those who are needy and promoting the work of sharing the message of God's love with others. By Jesus' own words this woman could be considered one of the needy for whom she was giving her offering. Yet she must have trusted that God would take care of her needs.

How do you feel about this woman's offering? How are you doing with submission and trust? Do you spend time and energy worrying about daily needs? Do you view what others have with jealousy and envy? Do you think it's possible to do either of those things and truly trust God to meet your basic needs? How would your life change if you could totally and completely trust God to meet your needs? The priority of what's truly important would change. Jealousy of what others have would change. Focus on God's priorities would take over. Difficult? Yes. Important? Yes. Will God help with the changes you need to make? Absolutely.

A HUMBLE HEART

Did the wealthy people in this story think they were being super generous? Perhaps they did. Perhaps they were. However it's also possible that they were giving for show ... to be seen ... to be admired ... to be celebrated for their generosity. Let's be honest. Many people (secretly) enjoy being noticed and celebrated for the things they do. They may be sincerely generous and happy to give their time or money but they kind of want people to notice what they are doing, even if they would never admit that. Remember that Jesus notices not just the gift of time or money but also what the heart is feeling about that gift.

Pride is a basic human emotion that you may battle on some level. Even if you say you want your gifts to be anonymous, it's always nice to get appreciation, at least from the recipient of your generosity. Maybe you're arguing with these words, saying that, "Yes you do like to give anonymously." That's great. The truth is that what you truly feel is between you and God. Just remember you can't fool Him. He sees your heart. Confessing your need for being noticed and submitting to God will give you a new beginning of humility before Him.

-DO-
justly

-LOVE-
mercy

-WALK-
humbly

MICAH 6:8

THE GOOD SAMARITAN

Based on Luke 10:30-37

THE GOOD SAMARITAN
Luke 10:30-37

Jesus told this story to show how to be a good neighbor:

A man was going from Jerusalem to Jericho when a band of robbers attacked him. They stripped off his clothes and beat him up then left him lying half dead on the side of the road. In a little while a priest came by and when he saw the poor man he crossed the street and kept on walking. Later a Levite — a Scripture teacher and a helper to the priest — came by. Just like the priest this man crossed the road to stay away from the injured man and he kept right on going.

Finally a Samaritan man came by (remember that Samaritans and Jews didn't like each other) and saw the man. He felt bad for him so he stopped and bandaged the man's wounds. He put the man on his donkey and then walked beside him to an inn where he took care of the man. The next day the Samaritan had to go about his business but he gave the innkeeper some money to look after the injured man. He promised to reimburse the innkeeper if there was more expense.

"Which one of these men was a neighbor to the injured man?" Jesus asked. Of course the right answer was that it was the man who took care of him.

LET GO OF PREJUDICES

The man who was attacked by the robbers certainly needed help. If anyone ever needed a new beginning, he did. He must have felt so hopeful when first the priest, then the Levite came by. He must have felt so abandoned when they kept right on walking. Did he expect anything from the Samaritan? Probably nothing good – maybe a kick in the stomach or something like that. Even though he may have felt true distaste for the Samaritans, this Jewish man must have been so grateful for the help.

Prejudices and pre-conceived opinions are very hard to let go of. Sometimes fear plays a role in that – fear of someone different. Sometimes arrogance plays a role – the belief that "my" way is the only right way. Do you struggle with any prejudices toward ethnic groups or people who adhere to a different lifestyle than you do? Are you judging others to the point that you cannot love them as Jesus taught? Perhaps you need a change in your heart so that you can love and serve as Jesus taught.

TOO IMPORTANT TO HELP

Who would be more likely to help a fellow human than a man whose life is devoted to serving God? That's what the injured man may have thought when he saw a priest coming toward him. What made the priest cross the road to avoid helping the man? Jesus doesn't give the reason. We can speculate, based on the ways people behave today. Perhaps the priest felt he was "above" the dirty work of helping a bloody, mostly naked man on the side of the road.

Is anyone too good or too important to care for another person? Shouldn't be, right? But for some reason certain people slide through life in difficult circumstances and few people pay any attention. Where are you on the "helping others" scale? There may be some folks you gladly help or serve. But are there others you tend to "cross the street to avoid"? Does your heart need to be softened toward a broader group of people? Do you need a heart change in serving?

NOTHING MORE IMPORTANT

The Levite was sort of the second level in temple leadership, just below the priest. He taught Scripture and assisted the priest as needed. So now the injured man has both of the important leaders of the temple come by but neither of them even comes close enough to see if he is still alive. Why did the Levite cross the road? Again, Jesus doesn't tell us the reason which, in itself, is kind of important. Jesus apparently felt there was no reason good enough to not help this poor man.

No reason is more important than caring for the people you meet. Did the Levite think he was too busy? Was he late for a meeting with the priest? Was he on assignment from the priest? Did he have an important class to teach? None of that should have mattered.

This example is mindful of the old saying, "Being so heavenly minded you are no earthly good." Are you so busy doing Christianity that you don't have time to BE Christian? Change that — put some white space in your life so that you have time for people. Jesus said, "Love God. Love others." That's what it's all about.

GETTING DIRTY

What was this guy thinking? He must have been on his way to some kind of appointment when he let an interruption stop his day. He may have gotten messy while cleaning the injured man's wounds. He put the man on his own donkey so he had to walk to get to the inn. He used his own materials to care for the man and spent his own money to pay the innkeeper, even promising to pay more if needed. AND he did all this for a man from a group of people he wasn't supposed to like. He definitely went above and beyond in his actions and care.

Perhaps something touches your heart so you toss a few dollars toward it so that someone else can do the work of getting dirty to help those who need it. Sometimes you agree to pray for a need because of course prayer is important but … could you put feet on the ground and work to help? Sometimes all you have to do is listen to someone who needs to share struggles.

Once again, Jesus said, "Love God. Love others." It shouldn't be hard. It will take time. It might take money. It might mean getting a little dirty. But it will be rewarding because it's what Jesus said to do.

SEEK THE
kingdom
-OF GOD ABOVE ALL ELSE-
live righteously
-AND HE WILL GIVE YOU-
everything
YOU NEED

MATTHEW 6:33

MARY
AND MARTHA

Based on Luke 10:38-42

MARY AND MARTHA
Luke 10:38-42

Jesus was friends with Mary, Martha and their brother, Lazarus. He probably visited often in their home when he was passing through town. This particular day Jesus and His friends stopped in and Martha probably greeted them then scurried off to prepare a fine meal for them. Her sister, Mary, greeted them, too, but instead of joining her sister in the kitchen, Mary sank down at Jesus' feet and listened to Him teach. Perhaps Martha kept peeking in, trying to catch Mary's eye and indicate she needed help. It never worked. Finally Martha, frustrated to the breaking point, marched in to Jesus and asked Him to tell Mary to go help her sister. She probably didn't expect the response she got from Him.

"Martha, you're worried about the wrong things," Jesus said. "Mary has chosen well and I will not take that away from her."

WHAT'S MOST IMPORTANT TO YOU?

Was it wrong that Martha wanted to prepare a nice meal for Jesus and His friends? Of course not. Over the years many women have felt bad for Martha. After all the preparations seem to have fallen totally on her shoulders. It wasn't fair, was it? Why didn't Jesus see that?

It's true there was nothing wrong with Martha wanting to serve a nice meal. The problem was in her priorities. Time with Jesus should have been more important to her than dinner. Jesus would have been happy with a cheese sandwich instead of duck à l'orange. He wanted Martha to sit down with Him and talk with Him and learn from Him.

Are you task oriented? Do you gain a sense of satisfaction from a job well done? There's nothing wrong with that unless your focus on completing tasks overshadows time spent with God or even with other people? What's most important? You've probably heard the statement that the thing you spend your time on is truly what's most important to you. Do you need to make some changes in your priorities? Do you need a new beginning?

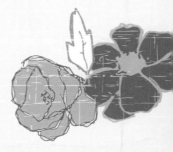

MARY MATTERED

Jesus broke apart some of the norms of the culture of His day. One of those breaks from accepted practices happened in this story. Jesus thought women were important. He thought it mattered that Mary chose to sit and listen to Him rather than do what was her expected role as a woman. He cared about her heart and soul even though she was female! His behavior, and He exhibited this care for women often, must have had an impact on His followers. Surely they noted that he considered women worth His time. Did that change their attitudes and behavior? We can only hope so.

Should His attitude affect yours? Absolutely. If you're female, celebrate that. Value your place in His work. Step forward and step up to do what Jesus has for you and to be the woman He has called you to be. If you've been dismissing yourself, put that behind you and step into a new beginning of placing as much value on YOU as Jesus does.

If you're male, value the women in your life — those in your family, ministry and workplace. Make sure they know you value them and respect them as equals. Follow Jesus' lead. You can't find a better example.

MARY LISTENED

Perhaps Mary was conflicted at first. After all, she knew her sister better than anyone. She knew Martha would expect her to help prepare the meal. She knew that was important to her sister. Did she weigh the costs in her mind ... listening to Jesus and feeling Martha's anger versus missing time with Jesus and helping her sister? Maybe she did. But she chose well. Jesus said so.

There is a constant battle in our lives between what's really important and the tyranny of the urgent. How often do we give in to the urgent instead of doing the important? It's a struggle for sure. But, according to what happened in this story, if we give in to the urgent and push away the important, we MISS the important. There's no denying the power of the urgent. It is a constant knocking on our heart's door. It's a steady infiltration of our thoughts. It's Satan trying to keep us away from God. If you're letting the urgent win most often – CHANGE your battle plan. Ask God to help you focus on Him and give you strength to take opportunities to be still and listen to Him. Jesus said Mary chose well. You want Him to say the same to you.

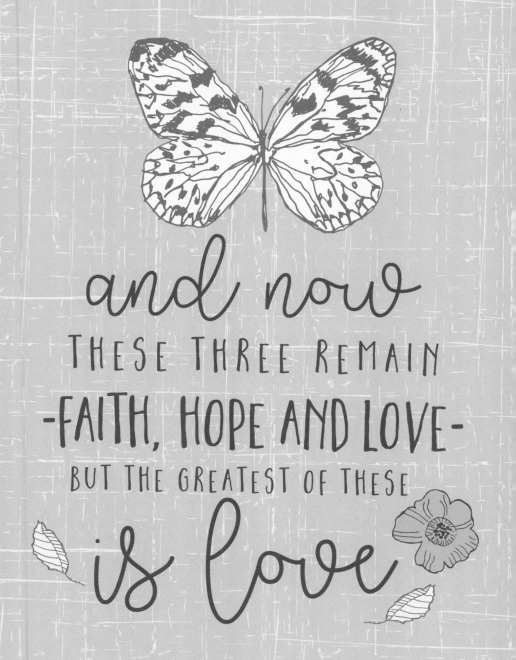

and now
THESE THREE REMAIN
-FAITH, HOPE AND LOVE-
BUT THE GREATEST OF THESE
is love

1 CORINTHIANS 13:13

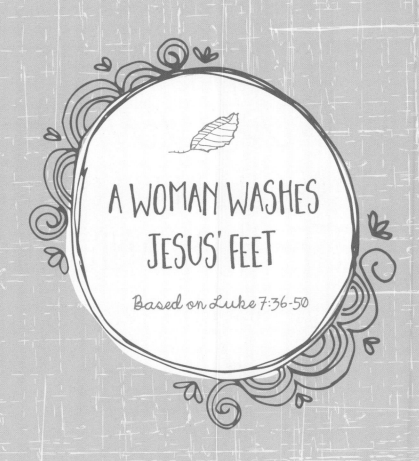

A WOMAN WASHES JESUS' FEET

Based on Luke 7:36-50

A WOMAN WASHES JESUS' FEET
Luke 7:36-50

Simon was a Pharisee who invited Jesus to his home for dinner. A sinful woman heard that Jesus was at Simon's home. She came there with an alabaster jar filled with expensive perfume. She fell to the floor at Jesus' feet and began crying. Her tears fell on His feet and she dried them with her long hair. Then, she kept crying as she poured the expensive perfume on His feet. Simon couldn't believe what he was seeing. He thought, "If Jesus is truly a prophet then He would know what kind of woman is touching Him!"

Jesus knew what Simon was thinking so He told him a story, "Two men owed a man some money. One owed him quite a lot, the other just a little. The man forgave both debts. Which one do you suppose loved the man most after that?"

"The one who was forgiven the larger debt," Simon answered.

"Right," Jesus said. "When I arrived, you didn't offer water that I might wash My feet. This woman has washed My feet with her tears. You didn't greet Me with a kiss but she has not stopped kissing my feet. You didn't anoint My head with oil but she has poured expensive perfume on my feet. She is indeed a sinful woman who has been forgiven all her sins and has shown Me great love. A person who is forgiven for a little loves only a little."

The men around the table wondered, "Who is this man who forgives sins?

Then Jesus told the woman, "Woman, your sins are forgiven. Go in peace."

A SINFUL WOMAN

Simon knew who this woman was. Perhaps the whole town knew of her. She had a reputation ... a label. This woman had apparently led a messed up life. No one cared what pushed her into her lifestyle choices. They just labeled her as a pretty hardcore sinner. As is often the case, labels are hard to escape. Maybe this was her first foray into being different. Maybe this was the moment she actually made her choice to change or at least made it public.

Imagine her tears as she sat at the feet of the One she knew could change her everything. Imagine the scent of the expensive perfume wafting through the room as she poured it on the feet of Jesus. Imagine the love filling her heart, running down her cheeks. Imagine a heart that knows it has been forgiven more than it deserves. Imagine a new beginning she never thought possible. Imagine.

Do you need a new beginning? Do you need to ask forgiveness and then accept it with all your heart – forgiving yourself because you know God has forgiven you? Then starting over – fresh and new because Jesus now lives in your heart? Imagine the possibilities!

THE LABEL HOLDERS

The religious elite had power. They surely had the power of holding the SINFUL WOMAN label tightly to the woman who was anointing Jesus. Simon was one of them. Once he had attached that label to her, he was not going to easily change his mind. He would need more proof than her tears and spilling out perfume that could have been sold to help the poor. He probably believed she was giving a pretty good performance.

Forgiveness and grace were not familiar words to Simon and those like him.

The world we live in is filled with people quick to pass judgments and paste labels on people – yes, even Christians. It's hard for people to get out from under those labels. They are expected to prove themselves over and over, and are not given the grace that others are offered.

Labeler or grace giver? If offering grace comes hard to you, it's time for a change. Ask God to help you offer grace as it's offered to you and to allow people to grow free of labels placed on them.

ARROGANT SELF-RIGHTEOUSNESS

Simon had been forgiven little. So, either he hadn't asked forgiveness for much or he hadn't sinned much. At any rate he didn't feel that he had been forgiven for much so that affected how he felt about the woman who anointed Jesus. Simon's self-righteousness made him arrogant and ungracious.

Those who think they are basically sin-free can be quite judgmental toward any they label as big-time sinners. They hold themselves above the sinners around them. Jesus pointed out that Simon had offered Jesus none of the common courtesies to a guest in his home. His behavior was not characteristic of someone seeking to share God's love with those around him. The woman's actions were loving and generous. Simon's arrogance betrayed the condition of his heart.

Do you need a change to take root in your heart? A change that will allow God to change self-righteousness in your heart to be changed into love and grace.

grace
-UPON-
grace

JOHN 1:16

ZACCHAEUS

Based on Luke 19

ZACCHAEUS
Luke 19

Zacchaeus was the chief tax collector and he was hated. He cheated people by charging them too much for taxes then keeping the extra money for himself. The people had no recourse against his dishonesty. News spread quickly that Jesus was coming to town and the road filled with people who wanted to see Him. Zacchaeus was curious about Jesus and he wanted to see Him, too. But Zacchaeus was a short man and by the time he got out to the crowded road he couldn't get to the front of the crowd where he would actually be able to see anything. None of the people would let him crowd to the front because no one liked him.

Then Zacchaeus had an idea. He saw a sycamore tree on the side of the road that had some low hanging branches. So he climbed up in the tree and watched as Jesus passed by below him. Jesus saw him and said, "Come down, Zacchaeus. I want to come to your house." The people criticized Jesus for going to eat with the hated tax collector.

But after Zacchaeus talked with Jesus he said, "I will give half of all my money to the poor. And, if I've cheated anyone I will pay them back four times what I took from them."

Jesus said, "Salvation has come to this man today."

ZACCHAEUS – BEYOND SAVING?

Zacchaeus was a sinner. He was a bad guy who had proven over and over that he was dishonest and didn't care who he stole from or who he hurt. Some people might have thought he was past being saveable. He was too wicked and too dishonest. No one would believe he was serious if he claimed to trust Jesus.

But no one is unsaveable. No sin is too great. It's never too late for a new beginning. After all, the thief on the cross had a new beginning just as he was dying. When a person comes into relationship with Jesus everything can change in a moment.

If you have been ignoring a mission field right in front of you because you have decided that a person is not saveable or would not be interested in God's love … change your attitude and trust God to do the heart changes.

MORE THAN REPENT

Zacchaeus was a dishonest tax collector. He stole from people who couldn't afford the basic taxes let alone the inflated amounts he required from them. He probably didn't even feel bad about cheating them. It was just what he did. He didn't mind that the people hated him. He didn't need them anyway.

But then he met Jesus and that experience changed his heart. He didn't just stop cheating people. He promised Jesus he would give half of his own money to help poor people. Then he would repay people he had cheated, not just what he had taken, but FOUR times what he had taken! Zacchaeus was a new man. Salvation had come to him.

Repent means to turn away from sin – stop doing it. So if you confess that you've wronged someone, you repent, you stop doing it. You don't do it again. Zacchaeus went farther than that and said he would give away money and repay people FOUR times what he had taken. His heart was truly changed. It was not enough to STOP cheating. He wanted to do more.

Repent ... turn away from sin. Go a changed-heart step further and make things right four times over!

REMEMBER JESUS' PURPOSES

The townspeople lined the road to see Jesus. They knew He claimed to be the Messiah. They knew He taught about God. They knew He was all about love and grace and forgiveness. But when they saw Him go home with Zacchaeus they criticized Him. They didn't think Jesus should spend time with such a terrible sinner. The amazing thing about that is that the people wanted Jesus to stay away from the person who most needed to meet Him.

Were they jealous of Zacchaeus getting personal time with Jesus? Did they think they deserved His attention? They seemed to have forgotten that Jesus was on earth with a purpose.

New beginnings always mean there was first an ending. In Zacchaeus' case, the ending was of something negative and the new beginning was positive. But the selfish people who thought they were better than the tax collector ignored their own sin of a judgmental spirit and forgetting Jesus' purpose and actually criticized the Savior.

Be careful what you criticize – especially if you're criticizing God for not giving the changes and new beginnings that you want. Remember His purposes.

HE PERFORMS *wonders* THAT CANNOT BE FATHOMED *miracles* THAT CANNOT BE COUNTED

JOB 5:9

JESUS FEEDS THE 5000

Based on John 6:1-13

JESUS FEEDS THE 5000
John 6:1-13

There was always a crowd of people following Jesus wherever He went. People wanted to see the miracles He did and perhaps get one for themselves. One day He and His disciples crossed the Sea of Galilee. Then they climbed up a hill and sat down. Jesus was going to teach His disciples but then He saw a big crowd of people crowding onto the hillside. They had found Him. Jesus turned to Philip and asked, "Where can we buy enough bread to feed all these people?" Philip was surprised that Jesus would even ask that because he knew that it would take a lot of money to feed the big crowd. Jesus already knew what He was going to do but He wanted to see what Philip would say.

Andrew overheard the question Jesus asked Philip and he said, "There's a boy in the crowd who has a lunch with him. It's small though – only five loaves of bread and two fish. That's not going to help much with this huge crowd."

"Get the boy's lunch and tell all the people to sit down," Jesus said. There were 5,000 men in addition to the women and children there on the hillside. Jesus took the bread and the fish and thanked God for them. Then He broke them into pieces and had the disciples hand them out to the crowd. Everyone had more than enough to eat. In fact, the disciples picked up twelve baskets full of leftovers!

165

THE WAYMAKER

Did Philip think Jesus was losing it when He asked how they could feed the massive crowd? Jesus had to know how much money it would take to buy food for all those people — money they didn't have. Did the disciples think Jesus had a plan? They had been with Him for a while. They had seen Him do miracles. They believed, at least on some level, that He was the Messiah. Yet it seemed like each time Jesus did something amazing, they were surprised. They just didn't quite get it. Did Jesus sometimes wonder when they were finally going to get "it"?

Do you think He ever wonders that about you? How long have you known Jesus? Do you spend time reading Scripture? Have you seen God move and guide in your life? Has He answered your prayers? Do you still wonder sometimes if He is hearing your prayers or if He is paying attention? Do you need a "new beginning" of a realization that He is indeed the Waymaker in your life — guiding and directing from His incredible love?

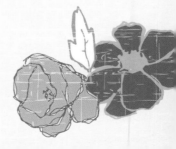

AN ORDINARY LUNCH

When the boy with the lunch left home that day he didn't know he was going to play a role in a miracle. He didn't know that all these years later we would still be talking about his lunch. It was just a lunch. He must have been amazed to see his simple lunch grow and grow and grow. Did Jesus' miracle that day change the boy? Probably so. How could it not? He got to play a part in an amazing miracle — one people are still talking about today!

What a wonderful example this miracle is of Jesus' care for the simple needs of life. He takes the most ordinary things and uses them in extraordinary ways. So you need never say, "I'm just me with no special talent or abilities. There's nothing special I can do for God." Don't say that — you never know what work He may have for you to be a part of or what simple thing (car, computer, lawnmower) you have that He may use to bless someone. Make today a new beginning and offer all you have and are to Him for His work.

BE AMAZED

Some of the crowd following Jesus probably wanted to hear His teaching. Some just hoped He would heal someone. Maybe they even brought a sick friend or family member with them. It's unlikely that they expected a free lunch; well lunch for 5000+ from just five loaves of bread and two fish. How amazing! You know how crowds of people react when they witness an incredible athletic act or anything that seems impossible. There are oooos and ahhhhs and cheers and head smacking – something was witnessed that no one thought they would ever see. For the rest of their lives people will recall the event and remember where they were and whom they were with when it happened. Those 5000+ people probably talked about that bread and fish lunch for the rest of their lives ... and that Jesus did it.

What do you feel when God surprises you? Does it take your breath away? Do you look up to the heavens and think, "I know that was YOU!" Or have you become a little jaded to God's work? Have you come to expect His everyday blessings? When He does something for you do you respond with, "OK. Good. Now on to the next thing ... ?" If that's happening way too often, STOP. Be amazed by your amazing God who loves you so much that He works in your life every moment of every day.

I WAIT FOR

the Lord

-MY WHOLE BEING WAITS-

AND IN HIS WORD

I PUT MY

hope

PSALM 130:5

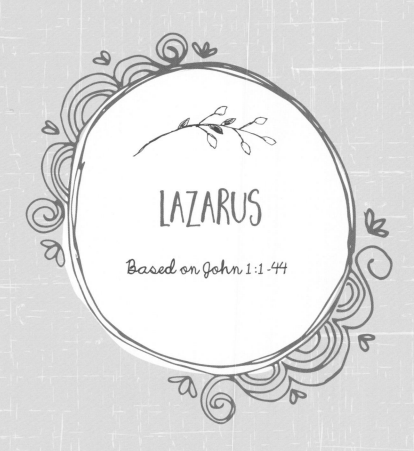

LAZARUS

Based on John 1:1-44

LAZARUS
John 11:1-44

Lazarus got sick and his sisters, Mary and Martha, sent for Jesus to come heal his friend. But Jesus waited two days then said He was going to Bethany. His disciples tried to stop Him because the people of Judea wanted to kill Jesus. It wasn't safe to go there. Finally Jesus said, "Our friend, Lazarus, is dead and for your sake I'm glad because now you may believe." So the disciples went along, expecting to die with Him in Judea.

When Jesus arrived, Lazarus had been buried four days. Many people were there comforting the sisters. Someone told Martha that Jesus was coming and she ran to meet Him. "If You had been here my brother wouldn't have died. But I know that God will give You whatever You ask for," she said.

"I am the resurrection and the life. Anyone who believes in Me will never die," Jesus said. "Martha, do you believe this?"

She said she did. Then Mary came and she also said, "My brother wouldn't have died if You had been here."

"Where is he?" Jesus asked. When they showed Him Lazarus' tomb He cried. "Move the stone," He said. But Martha reminded Him that Lazarus' body would smell terrible.

Jesus said, "Didn't I tell you that if you believed you would see the power of God?" So they moved the stone and Jesus prayed, "Father, thank You for always hearing Me." Then He called, "Lazarus, come out!"

Lazarus walked out of the tomb!. "Take off the grave clothes," Jesus said. "He is alive!"

DISCIPLES TAKE A STAND

The disciples were looking out for Jesus. They knew that His popularity was rising which meant that there were people who wanted Him out of the way — dead. When they suggested that it wasn't a good idea to go back to Judea right now they were sincere in reminding Him of the danger. Of course, He went. AND … they went along, expecting to die with Him in Judea. That's devotion; sacrificial devotion that grows from love and trust.

Through the years believers have had to make the choice to believe to the point of death. They give up their lives by taking a stand for their faith in God. Of course that takes them into a new beginning of eternal life and they are surely greeted by the Father's words, "Well done, My faithful servant."

You may never be asked to die for your faith but you are undoubtedly offered opportunities to deny Christ or take a stand for Him by the way you live, speak, relate to others, opinions you voice and decisions you make. Are you willing to take a stand for Him? It's not always easy, but would be a change in your heart that honors Him.

LAZARUS' FRIENDSHIP WITH JESUS

Well you can't get any more of a new beginning than Lazarus got! Restored life … life! There are two important parts to this story – Lazarus, of course, is one. He was a friend of Jesus. So he had a relationship with Jesus before the death/resurrection part of the story. He took the time that it takes to be a friend.

The second part of the story to recognize is that Jesus waited until Lazarus had died to go to him because He wanted His disciples to witness this miracle. He said He was doing this so they would believe. It was an object lesson like no other that Jesus is the resurrection and the life.

The "so what" of this story for today's readers is the importance of relationship with Jesus. Time spent with Him deepens the friendship and trust. No doubt Lazarus spent the rest of his life, his second life, following Jesus. It's also important to note that some of the experiences you have to go through, as difficult as they are, may be happening so that you learn and grow deeper in your faith. Jesus wants that change in you – deeper, fuller dependence on Him.

MARY AND MARTHA

We know a little more about these sisters than just this story. Mary is the one who sat at Jesus' feet, crying and pouring expensive perfume on them then wiping them with her hair. She loved Jesus deeply. Martha loved Him, too, but she could get caught up in the tasks before her and they became more important than listening to Him teach.

However both sisters believed that Jesus could have saved their brother if He had come before Lazarus died. They trusted His power. So what did they need to learn? Perhaps it was the realities of Jesus' power over death. That not even death stops Him from doing what He wants.

Mary and Martha seem to be two distinct personalities. Both of them learned an incredible lesson of just what Jesus had been teaching — He IS the resurrection and the life. Those who believe in Him WILL live forever. Not even death has power over Him. Mary and Martha may have known that in their minds but after their brother came back to life they knew it in their hearts, too.

Does the prospect of eternal life with Jesus warm your heart? Are you excited to be with Him and with loved ones who have gone to heaven already? Jesus promised it. It will be the last new beginning for you!

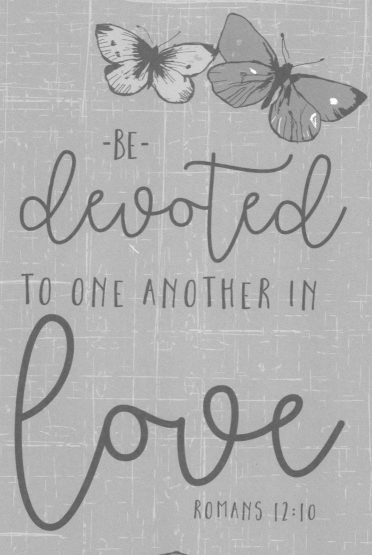

-BE-
devoted
TO ONE ANOTHER IN
love
ROMANS 12:10

THE STORY OF DORCAS

Based on Acts 9:36-43

THE STORY OF DORCAS
Acts 9:36-43

Everyone knew Dorcas. She was one of the nicest women ever. She constantly did kind things for others, especially for the poor. So of course when Dorcas got sick and died, her friends were very sad. They tended to her body and prepared it for burial. But then they heard that Peter was in a nearby town. They knew that he followed Jesus and had witnessed many of the miracles Jesus had done. They sent a couple of men to beg Peter to come and help them.

When Peter arrived Dorcas's friends gathered around him and told of all the wonderfully kind things she had done for them. The widows tearfully showed him some of the clothing she had made for them. Peter asked them all to leave the room then he knelt next to Dorcas's body and prayed. After he prayed he said, "Dorcas, get up." Immediately Dorcas opened her eyes and sat up and Peter helped her get up. Then he called in all of her friends and gave them back their friend!

Of course the news of this miracle spread through the town very quickly and many people believed in the Lord because of it.

DORCAS'S NEW START IN NEW LIFE

Dorcas showed what kind of person she was in the way she lived her life. Her kindness and generosity endeared her to everyone who knew her. So, of course, her sudden death made her friends very sad as well as the poor widows she had been so generous to. But they weren't sad just because their benefactor had died. They were truly sorry that their friend was gone.

Dorcas's new start in life was her new life which grew from her generous and kind treatment of others. Because of her love for them, her friends loved her in return and wanted her back. They were instrumental in getting Peter to come help them.

People make a difference. You are not meant to go through life alone. Are you kind, generous and helpful to others? Are you building relationships with those around you? Do you have a tribe of friends who will help you and be there for you when you have a need and to whom you can do the same? Make relationships a new priority in your life today.

FRIENDS MAKE A DIFFERENCE

Dorcas's friends were the best! They didn't take her death as a final answer. They believed that Peter could ask God to give life back to her and that God would listen to Peter. They had to try. Their efforts to intervene on behalf of their friend paid off. The benefit for them was that they got their friend back.

It's a privilege to be the friend who intervenes in prayer on behalf of someone else. Change or a new beginning may not come for that friend without someone to intervene in prayer or in physical help. Bonds are built between people when they pray for one another and share their most vulnerable needs. When you experience change that takes you to a hard place, as Dorcas experienced, you find that everything is stripped away except God and your friends who will intervene on your behalf.

-FOR WITH GOD-

nothing

SHALL BE

impossible

LUKE 1:37

SAUL'S CONVERSION

Based on Acts 9

SAUL'S CONVERSION
Acts 9

Saul wanted to get rid of Christians. He tossed them in jail whenever he could. He took care of the Christians in Jerusalem and headed to Damascus to do the same. He was walking along the road with some men when a bright light shone down on him. Saul fell down as a voice said, "Saul, why are you persecuting Me?"

"Who are you?" Saul asked.

"Jesus. The one you are persecuting," Jesus answered. "Get up and go into the city. You'll be told what to do after that."

The men with Saul didn't know what was happening. They heard the voice but they didn't see anyone. When Saul got up he couldn't see. His eyes had a crust on them. So the men had to take his hand and lead him into town. For three days he couldn't see and he didn't eat or drink anything.

Meanwhile God spoke to a Christian in Damascus named Ananias. "Go to a house on Straight Street and ask for a man named Saul. He has been told to expect you."

Ananias was scared because of Saul's reputation. "Lord, that man came here to arrest Christians. You don't really want me to go to him, do You?"

God said, "I have work for him to do." When Ananias went to Saul and touched him Saul could see again. He was baptized and began preaching about Jesus right away. Because of Saul, whose name was changed to Paul, many people believed in Jesus and grew strong in their faith.

A PASSIONATE NEW MAN

Saul was not a nice guy and he was very passionate in his hatred of Christians. God used an extreme method to get Saul's attention. It worked and Saul believed that Jesus was truly God's Son and His work was real. He had three days of fasting to think things through in darkness and when Ananias came and Saul's sight was restored, he hit the ground running — a new man. He was just as passionate about sharing Jesus as he had been about fighting Jesus.

Are you passionate about your faith? Or have you lost some of your spiritual vim and vigor as life has gotten busier? Did you start your walk with Christ with energy and enthusiasm but have now fallen into a doldrum? It's time for a reawakening, a reinvigorating, a new beginning of passion to share the love of God with the world so that all may know Him!

THE INFLUENCE OF ANANIAS

You can understand Ananias' hesitancy to go see Saul. He knew that Saul was coming to Damascus to throw people like Ananias in jail. How did he know that this wasn't some scheme to get Christians close to him? But when God said, "No, Saul's My man," Ananias went. He trusted God and he did exactly what God asked him to do.

God sometimes asks His followers to go into difficult situations, even some which are dangerous. His plan involves a bigger picture than the immediate instance. Nothing in God's work is wasted. So when Ananias did what God asked him to do, he may have been frightened but he knew that God had a reason and his visit with Saul was part of a bigger plan.

That visit with Saul opened new beginnings in his life and work. He was baptized and began a long, fruitful ministry for God.

Having the opportunity to feed into another person's life is exciting and you may plan a part in a bigger ministry than you ever dreamed. Take a chance, even if it's on something scary. If God sends you, He will go with you and you have no idea how far He will take your influence.

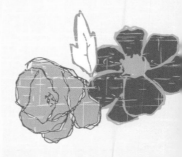

THE GROWING CHURCH

God's plan was to grow the church beyond the original Jewish Christians. He wanted the Gentiles to hear the message of His love. Paul was going to be God's messenger to begin the process of the Gentiles hearing about God. Of course, the church grew and grew as Paul preached and taught. He planted churches and then wrote letters to those churches to continue teaching them about living for God. Those letters are now part of our Bible so we can continue learning from Paul.

Saul/Paul's new beginning is still affecting believers today because of the presence of his letters in the Bible. These letters were not just Paul's words, but God speaking through him. Scripture itself tells us it is important to know God's Word. Psalm 119:105 says, "Your word is a lamp to guide my feet and a light for my path." Memorizing God's Word so it is hidden in your heart for any time you might need it will change your life!

WHERE GOD
guides
HE
provides

ISAIAH 58:11

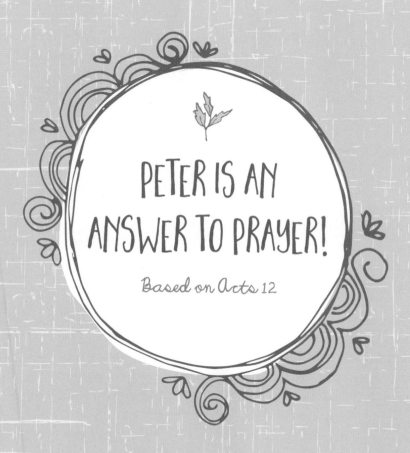

PETER IS AN ANSWER TO PRAYER!

Based on Acts 12

PETER IS AN ANSWER TO PRAYER!
Acts 12

King Herod had Peter arrested and planned a public trial right after Passover. He threw him in prison, guarded by four squads of four soldiers each. While Peter was securely locked up the church prayed fervently for his release.

The night before the trial was to happen, Peter was sleeping while chained between two soldiers with two chains. Guards were at the door of his cell. Suddenly an angel nudged Peter awake and told him to get up and get dressed. The chains holding Peter to the guards just fell off! "Follow me," the angel said. The door of the cell opened and they walked past the guards who didn't seem to see them. Peter didn't know whether he was dreaming or what. The angel led him out of the prison then disappeared. Peter realized then that God had sent His angel to free him.

Peter hurried to the house where he knew people would be praying for him. When he got there he knocked on the door and a servant girl named Rhoda asked who was outside. Peter answered her and she was so excited to hear his voice that she forgot to open the door. She ran to tell the people that Peter was at the door. They had been praying for his safety but couldn't believe he was actually at the door. They thought it must be his angel. Meanwhile Peter was still knocking! Finally they opened the door and saw that it was indeed Peter. God had answered their prayer!

ELEVENTH HOUR ANSWERS

Peter was in big trouble. King Herod was going to make God's enemies happy by putting Peter on trial and possibly condemn him to death. Herod had already murdered James, another of Jesus' followers. Now he had Peter securely chained and guarded so there would be no chance of his escape.

There was no hope, right? No one could break in and Peter couldn't break out. Actually, there's always hope when God is involved. God had more work for Peter to do. He wasn't ready for Peter to die so He sent His angel and set Peter free.

Are you facing situations that seem hopeless? Health? Career? Relationships? Ministry? Are you wondering how things can possibly change? Never give up. God may surprise you! This story is an example of God's plan and power. He can change your situation and if you pray for that and wait on His timing, He will. Peter's change was at the 11th hour – just in time! God is in control ... no matter what. Trust Him. Follow Him. Thank Him. Do what He directs you to do.

HALLELUJAH JOY!

Rhoda was just a servant. Was she also a Christian? Possibly. For sure she had heard the people in the house praying for Peter's safety. They were praying passionately, calling out to God to intervene and save the life of their friend. So when there was a knock on the door, Rhoda crept silently to answer, careful not to disturb the prayer meeting. She didn't open the door without asking who was outside. That wouldn't have been safe considering the king's attitude toward Christ followers. But when Peter identified himself, she was so filled with "Hallelujah joy" that she ran to tell the praying people that their prayers were answered! But … she forgot to open the door.

Hallelujah joy! God answered your prayer! He has changed the obvious of what was going to happen. He made a new beginning. He did what God does! Don't forget to "open the door" to celebrate His work in changing and making new beginnings. Step in!

PRAYERS ANSWERED

The Christians prayed. They prayed a lot. They prayed fervently. They were first generation Christians. Many of them had heard Jesus teach. They may have seen His miracles. They were led by men and women who were personal followers and friends of Jesus. They knew God heard their prayers and believed He would answer. They had seen it happen. So when James was murdered by Herod and Peter was arrested, they gathered to pray for his safety.

But when Rhoda told them that Peter was knocking on the door, their immediate response was, "No way. It can't be Peter. It must be his angel." They thought he was already dead.

Of course when they discovered that Peter was indeed free, they must have been filled with awe. God had answered their prayers — even while they prayed! That must have strengthened their faith in Him. It must have encouraged them to pray for more needs and expect His answers.

When something changes in your life or situation and you know it could only have happened by God's hand, let it grow your faith and your awareness that He is paying attention to your life and is hearing your prayers. Each time you see Him working, you can be reminded of His love and your faith in Him grows deeper.

BYSTANDER HEART CHANGES?

The soldiers who guarded Peter worked for King Herod. They did what he told them to do. More than likely doing anything else would get them killed. So they chained themselves to the prisoner. They locked the door and stood guard outside it. There was NO WAY they were going to let Peter escape! Except … he did because when God wants something to happen, it does!

Did the soldiers get in trouble because he escaped? Probably. But, what about in that moment when they knew they had done everything they could; everything they were supposed to do; but Peter was gone anyway. Did they recognize that God's power is greater than Herod's was? Did they, in that moment believe in His power and plan? We never know what's going on in the hearts and minds of non-Christians when they see God moving in our lives. Hopefully their hearts are changing.

Don't discount what change may happen in the hearts of scoffers around you. When people see answers to prayer; God's miraculous work in your life, speak up and give Him credit! Let it be known that all glory goes to Him and pray for heart changes in the lives of those who need to recognize God's greatness, power and love.